All contents copyright © 2014 by Amy Roberts
2nd Edition copyright © 2018
All rights reserved.
No part of this document or the related links may be reproduced or redistributed in any form, by any means (electronic, photo-copying, or otherwise) without the prior written permission of the author.
Amy Roberts
amy@raisingarrows.net

ABOUT THE AUTHOR

Amy Roberts is the homeschooling mother of 7 living children and one precious little girl named Emily being held in the Lord's arms.

She never set out to be a mom of many, nor a homeschooling mom of many. She hadn't prepared for this all her life. She didn't have a hope chest filled with Large Family Recipes or Homeschooling How-To's. She was just an ordinary gal, put in extraordinary circumstances in order that her life would bring glory to an Almighty God.

This book is the natural outcropping of a website (RaisingArrows.net) dedicated to helping ordinary moms live extraordinary lives in Christ by surrendering everything.

It is her deepest prayer that within the pages of this book you will find the encouragement and skills you need to homeschool your large family for God's glory!

TABLE OF CONTENTS

NOTE ABOUT THE COVER		**1**
INTRODUCTION		**3**
THE HEART STUFF		**5**
CHAPTER 1	Act Like a Large Family {Before You Are One}	**6**
CHAPTER 2	Learn to Love Your Children	**10**
CHAPTER 3	Enough of You to Go Around?	**14**
CHAPTER 4	Heart-schooling - The Art of Mothering	**27**
THE PRACTICAL STUFF		**37**
CHAPTER 5	Herding Cats: How to Combat the Chaos	**38**
CHAPTER 6	Keeping it Clean	**49**
CHAPTER 7	Organizing the Large Family Homeschool	**58**

CHAPTER 8	Getting Your Homeschool Day Started Off On the Right Foot	67
CHAPTER 9	Homeschooling from the Bottom to the Top	71
CHAPTER 10	Corporate Homeschooling	75
CHAPTER 11	Chunk Learning	89
CHAPTER 12	Training Toward Independence	93
CHAPTER 13	Keeping Track of it All: Planning & Record-Keeping	99
THE EXTRA STUFF		**106**
CHAPTER 14	Lighting Fires	107
CHAPTER 15	Extra-Curricular Activities	112
CHAPTER 16	Large Family Fun	119
CHAPTER 17	Affording the Large Family Homeschool	123
CHAPTER 18	Feeding the Crew	128
THE OTHER STUFF		**138**
CHAPTER 19	Caring for Yourself (and what about "Me Time"?)	139
CHAPTER 20	Homeschooling with Morning Sickness	145

CHAPTER 21	Homeschooling with a Newborn	**149**
CHAPTER 22	Homeschooling with a Toddler	**168**
CHAPTER 23	Homeschooling During Crisis	**175**
EPILOGUE	What I Wish Someone Had Told Me About Homeschooling	**188**
APPENDIX	Homeschooling Methods & Large Family Considerations	**194**
	Cherish Your Children Checklist	**203**
	Age-Appropriate Chore List	**205**
RESOURCES		**210**

Large Family Homeschooling Book Resource Page:
https://www.raisingarrows.net/lfhresources

NOTE ABOUT THE COVER

You may look at the cover of *Large Family Homeschooling* and wonder why there are "only" 4 children on the cover. This was done purposefully.

Long ago, a friend told me that 4 children was a large small family and 5 children was a small large family. However, the birth of my 4th child marked a "crossover point" for me; a point where everything changed. It was at this number that I had to learn how to cook, clean, and school differently. And there were many, many days when four children felt like a huge family! I now have twice that many children. Four children would seem like an empty house to me! But I have not forgotten those days when having 4 children changed my world. That is why the cover of this book has "only" 4 children.

And while I do not believe there is a magic number where you stop being a small family and start being a large family, I do believe that homeschooling 4 children looks very different from homeschooling 3 children.

I also firmly believe you can successfully apply many of the ideas and methods from this book with a family of less than 4 children, so don't think you aren't allowed to read this book unless you "qualify"! God led you to this book for a reason. May you be blessed by what you find here!

INTRODUCTION

Once upon a time, I didn't have a large family. I had an average-sized family. One mom, one dad, one boy, one girl, one cat. We were about as nuclear as you could get.

Growing up, I thought having lots of children sounded like fun, but that was mostly because I grew up without siblings close in age and I longed for what I didn't have. BUT...once I realized how much work went into just one child, I decided one was enough. My husband talked me into another baby a couple of years later, and with the birth of our daughter, we officially had the "perfect family".

But, God had other plans.

He put us on a wild and wonderful path toward a household full of children and full of love, and while I could talk for days about how great having a large family is, this book is not about that. This book is written with the assumption you already have a large family or want one and you homeschool or you want to in whatever combination of those you happen to be in right now. This book is not only the nuts and bolts of large family homeschooling, but the heart of it as well. By the time you finish reading this book, I pray you feel encouraged and inspired!

The Heart Stuff

CHAPTER 1

Act Like a Large Family (Before You Are One)

Why You Shouldn't Stress About Homeschool Planning

I am starting here because many of you reading this are not yet a large family, but you hope to be someday. Even if you never make it to that "official" large family status, living life the large family way will benefit you tremendously.

Our family adopted a large family mentality long before we were a large family. That fact alone, revolutionized our home life. Ever since then, I've found it important to tell other families how organizing, structuring, and managing a home in the same way a large family would will positively impact their lives.

Why I adopted a large family mentality:
It happened simply because I began to desire a large family. Because of this desire, I began frequenting large family sites on the internet and the real-life homes of people who had large families. I observed. I asked questions. I mimicked.

What happened when I adopted a large family mentality?:
I had two children and my husband was deployed during the timeframe I began to adopt a large family mentality, so the most obvious difference was that my day was much more streamlined and easier to manage. The second thing I noticed was that my children were happier. I also realized I was more content and relaxed as well.

Where did I start?:
I started with a Bath Routine. It was a simple place to start and easy to implement. I bathed my two children on Tuesday night, Thursday night, and Saturday night.

CHAPTER 1

From there, I learned to menu plan, clean, and homeschool all based on the mentality that I needed to be efficient and organized.

What types of large family things can a small family implement?: Just about anything! I'd encourage you to peruse the Large Family section of Raising Arrows, and also consider these things...

- **Share bedrooms** - Large families do this because they have to, but it builds such camaraderie between siblings, I suggest it to everyone.

- **Color Code** - Some families color code everything (towels, notebooks, cups, etc), but we choose only to color code the things we find most often cause chaos in our home. For us, this means chore charts, notebooks and our DrinkBands for our cups. Color coding builds efficiency in any size household because you can quickly see what belongs to whom.

- **Give the Children Chores** - Require work from them. This builds responsibility and character and teaches them that a household is held together by the entire family and not just one person. Children are capable of so much more than we give them credit for.

In the Appendix of this book, you will find an Age-Appropriate Chore List to help you start the process of assigning chores.

Why You Shouldn't Stress About Homeschool Planning

- **Streamline Everything!** - The more efficient you become, the more time you have for your family. Start with a problem area in your home and brainstorm ways to make things run smoother there. This will forever be a work-in-progress because life changes and problem areas change with it, but keep after it, always tweaking to make things more efficient and easier to manage.

- **See Your Children as Blessings** - Start enjoying your children for who God made them to be. Revel in their crooked smiles and open-mouthed kisses. See them as God sees them...not as something you must do for the next 18 years, but as someone you've been blessed with for an eternity. While not all large families feel blessed by their little ones, a fair share hold fast to the truth of Psalm 127 in which God calls children a reward and a blessing. When God says something, believe it!

You know, maybe we should talk about the reward and blessing of children just a bit more...

CHAPTER 2

Learn to Love Your Children

Learn to Love Your Children

Lo, children are an heritage of the LORD: and the fruit of the womb is his reward. As arrows are in the hand of a mighty man; so are children of the youth. Happy is the man that hath his quiver full of them: they shall not be ashamed, but they shall speak with the enemies in the gate.
Psalm 127:3-5

The title of this chapter might surprise you. But, as someone who spent the first several years of her mothering feeling un-blessed, I know that sometimes you have to actually learn how to feel blessed and learn how to love your children. But lest you think I made this up, read this passage of Scripture:

...and so train the young woman to love their husbands and children.
Titus 2:4

To "train" someone to do something means to teach them to go against their natural inclinations. Our natural inclination as human beings tends toward the selfish side. We must LEARN to love our children despite our selfish tendencies.

It took a complete change of heart for me to see my family and my home as a blessing...a change of heart only God could have given. I had to learn to not only LOVE my family, but to LIKE my family.

I had to learn to feel blessed.

CHAPTER 2

When the Lord placed Psalm 127 in front of me and opened my eyes to its words, I remember spending hours pondering the notion that children are a blessing and a reward. I certainly did not treat them that way. In fact, I was almost convinced my then 3 year old son was the naughtiest child on the planet and spent his waking hours crafting up ways to terrorize our home.

Looking back, I realized he wasn't naughty at all.

He was 3.

I had expectations that were so outrageous and unattainable for my children, that there was absolutely no way they could ever meet them to my satisfaction. I didn't feel blessed because I didn't recognize my blessings.

How easy it is to focus on the negative. We see only that which distresses us. We keep meticulous records of wrongs and then wonder why our home feels tense and troubled.

We must turn from this way of life and begin to see the blessings before us!
But how?
I'm getting ready to say something shocking. Brace yourself.

Fake it.

Learn to Love Your Children

If you don't feel blessed, pretend like you do. You have practiced being UNblessed for how many ever years you've been a mother and now it is a habit. But habits can change. Trust me. It may feel incredibly awkward to act blessed {at first}, especially if your oldest child is jr. high age or older, but the more you practice it {even when you don't feel like it}, the more you begin to feel truly blessed. This is a change of heart and mind, but remember, the Lord is fully capable of bringing this about.

Do not be conformed to this world, but be transformed by the renewal of your mind, that by testing you may discern what is the will of God, what is good and acceptable and perfect.
Romans 12:2

You aren't doing this on your own. You have Christ working in you and through you. Relationships can be built and even restored.

Start practicing being blessed right now! Start cherishing those blessings the Lord has given to you!

In the Appendix of this book, you will find a Cherish Your Children Checklist to help you learn to love and be blessed by your children.

CHAPTER 3

Enough of You to Go Around?

Enough of You to Go Around?

When you walk into a grocery store with a trail of children behind you, you make a scene. Often, complete strangers will come up to you and ask rather pointed questions. The most common question I get is,

How do you do it?

Everyone who asks me that typically feels as if they are drowning in the parenting of two children, and the thought of more than that scares them. When they find out we homeschool, that pretty much brings them to their knees.

But, the fact of the matter is, I didn't suddenly wake up one day with 8 children. I had them one at a time. I added them to our homeschool one at a time. (If I ever have twins, I will have to amend that statement!)

And I started homeschooling LONG before I had a lot of kids.

I've been homeschooling from the beginning. My son was 4 ½ when I started him in what could have been considered Kindergarten. He was a smart cookie (still is!) and I was excited to be teaching him.

Truth be told, I hadn't always wanted to homeschool. In fact, for most of my son's little life I had been looking forward to someone else teaching him! But there is something about realizing your children are blessings that makes you WANT to be around them, and I wanted to be around him all day, every day.

CHAPTER 3

Little did I know where God was leading me. As the years progressed, I caught a vision for homeschooling, and as our family grew, I added each child in with excitement. I still get excited every time a new little one "officially" joins our homeschool day.

> *{Note from Amy – Our Homeschool Story}*
> *People are often curious about why I homeschool. As I mentioned above, I didn't set out to homeschool, but ended up there through circumstances only the Lord could have orchestrated. My husband was deployed with Operation Enduring Freedom and Operation Noble Eagle one right after the other. That same year, our local public school decided to go to all-day Kindergarten. We couldn't bear the thought of sending our son away from mommy all day under the strain of not having daddy in the home either.*
>
> *Our pastor's family did this strange thing called homeschooling, so I asked them more about it, and decided I could surely handle doing something like that while my husband was away from us.*
>
> *The rest is history. I fell in love with my children all over again. There is something about teaching them at home that opens your eyes to the blessings they truly are. There is very much to be said about spending QUANTITY time with your children and not just quality time. And as I also said above, I caught the vision of homeschooling as a way to disciple and lead those children entrusted to our care. There was no way I was going to waste that opportunity!*

Enough of You to Go Around?

> *Your story is undoubtedly very different from mine, but I am sure you can look back and see the hand of God in it as well. I would encourage you to tell your children those stories. It is part of their heritage and they need to know this homeschooling thing isn't something random in their lives.*

Perhaps as your family grows, you wonder how there will ever be enough of you to go around? Let me be perfectly candid with you:

Sometimes there isn't.

There are days when to rise above the clatter, I have to yell. {That makes absolutely no sense, but I do it anyway—and we all have a good laugh over the ridiculousness of it.}

There are days when everyone's emergency becomes my crisis.

There are days when I wonder how my sophomore will get into college, if my 7th grader will ever realize math is not her mortal enemy, how my 1st grader will ever learn to read fluently, when my preschooler will stop tackling his younger brother every chance he gets, if my toddler will ever stop eating chapstick, and if the baby will someday stop needing me to carry him everywhere.

It is on those days I wonder if there really is enough of me to go around. Am I somehow cheating my children out of a normal life? Is all this sharing and waiting their turn somehow bad for them?

CHAPTER 3

I also wonder when I'll get my act in gear and grow up. You know, the kind of "grown up" who lives a life without hitches, hiccups, or help.

But God is merciful to meet me at the edge and remind me that what he has called me to, He will equip me for.

Now may the God of peace who brought again from the dead our Lord Jesus, the great shepherd of the sheep, by the blood of the eternal covenant, equip you with everything good that you may do his will, working in us that which is pleasing in his sight, through Jesus Christ, to whom be glory forever and ever. Amen.
Hebrews 13:21

I didn't randomly decide one day to have as many children as I could. That was God. He's given each of these children to me, and as they are added, He adds the grace I need to love and care for them. But I will never be enough.

I don't homeschool because I think I'm some great teacher. That was God too. As each child is added to our homeschool schedule, God is faithful to focus my heart and mind on Him and what His schedule for my family consists of.

I have been called to a life that is very different from the one I had all neatly laid out, but God is not going to leave me to muddle through all by myself. I may not be "enough," but He is! God hasn't asked me to do it all. He's asked me to give my all... to Him. He'll order my life from there. All I have to do is live it.

Enough of You to Go Around?

The days when I feel stretched thin, bogged down, and bent out of shape are usually the days when in an effort to control my environment, I lose sight of the things that truly matter. God's ways aren't always my ways, but God is always right.

In order to have enough of me to go around, I have to let go of some of my expectations. I have to let God lead. I have to be content with his Light only shining on my very next step, rather than the entire path.

So, now that you understand that "enough of me" really isn't an issue, let's dig into some practical ways to "stretch" yourself as you homeschool your large family:

Plan the Work, Work the Plan
Planning is an important part of homeschooling. It is difficult to do a good job without some semblance of planning and scheduling. In a large family, you have to plan the work and work the plan or you will end up with utter chaos.

That said, often the plan isn't fully realized. We'll talk more about this in Chapter 13, but let me give you a quote from Dwight D. Eisenhower that sums up how I feel about plans and schedules:

"Plans are useless, but planning is indispensable."
~Dwight D. Eisenhower

So, while you really need to plan, don't let the plan rule you.

CHAPTER 3

If your day doesn't go as planned and you end up a mess, you are misusing your schedules and planning. You are letting them rule you, rather than mastering them and using them as tools to help you run your homeschool.

So while a good schedule can actually add time to your day, you have to be flexible in order to take care of off-schedule items. When you have off-schedule items, make a list of those things and work through the list in an orderly fashion, making the rest of your schedule fit around the list. Avoid throwing the schedule out completely because every single day has its share of off-schedule items, especially in a large family! If you start throwing out your schedule every time you have something extra to fit in, you'll never utilize your schedule and you'll always feel off track.

Delegate
You are the manager of your home and homeschool, and good managers ALWAYS delegate responsibilities.

Moms have this notion they should be able to do everything and be everything to everybody. That is a complete and utter lie. The Bible is quite clear about our unique giftings within the church. This most certainly extends into our family and homeschool.

For the body does not consist of one member but of many. If the foot should say, "Because I am not a hand, I do not belong to the body," that would not make it any less a part of the body. And if the ear should say, "Because I am not an eye, I do not belong to

Enough of You to Go Around?

the body," that would not make it any less a part of the body. If the whole body were an eye, where would be the sense of hearing? If the whole body were an ear, where would be the sense of smell? But as it is, God arranged the members in the body, each one of them, as he chose. If all were a single member, where would the body be?
1 Corinthians 12: 14-19

Learn your limitations and learn to delegate. But, who do you delegate to?

Surprisingly, there are a lot of options here. The first one that comes to mind are grandparents, and I'm not talking about having the grandparents actually take over the teaching, but rather giving them opportunities to facilitate some of the learning. For instance, when they come for a visit, have them read stories to the children or even let your new readers try reading to them. Have the children share their work with the grandparents and listen as the grandparents tell stories from their school years. Ask Grandma to show the children how to address an envelope or ask Grandpa to read off spelling words for a pop quiz. Grandparents are also great for helping with those little extras that are hard to fit into a day, like a tea party or a nature walk. It's a win-win-win situation!

You can also delegate to the children themselves. We'll talk more about this in Chapter 12, but we all know how important it is to give children responsibilities as they age. Their homeschooling is no different. Children need to be given a love to learn and allowed to take flight with that love. Let them

CHAPTER 3

research, let them plan their own work, let them keep track of their grades and their schedules as they get older.

> *{Note from Amy - Training for Excellence}*
> *Train your children to do jobs correctly from the start. I could have saved myself numerous hours of training and retraining had I been diligent in the beginning days of teaching a new responsibility.*
>
> *How do you do this?*
>
> *Show them how.*
> *Work alongside them.*
> *Stand over them while they try it themselves.*
> *Let them try without you.*
> *Check their work.*
> *Have them redo anything they missed.*
>
> *Be gentle and patient. It will pay off!*

How about delegating some things to Dad? There are many women who complain about Dad not pitching in with things, but men aren't always in tune with the family's day-to-day life and need a little briefing on where they can pitch in at. Perhaps Dad can help out with science projects? Maybe he can help via text messages or phone calls during the day. Maybe he can do Bible time before or after work. Don't be pushy, but do ask. And don't forget to bounce ideas off of him when you are feeling overwhelmed. Brainstorm with him ways you can hand off some of the load you carry.

Enough of You to Go Around?

Eliminate your time wasters
Another way to gain back some time is to get rid of the unnecessary things that are eating your time.

My time wasters have changed over the years. When my older children were small my biggest time waster was sewing. It seemed like a noble thing, but all too often I didn't keep it in its proper place. Now my biggest time waster is that big, bad internet! Whenever I start to see my productivity and time wane, it is almost always due to too much time spent online.

If you feel crunched for time, then there's a good chance there is something in your life that needs to go. I would encourage you to keep a log of your day for a few days and see where your time is going. Be honest, not perfect. I think you will quickly see what it is that needs to be either eliminated completely or at the very least, scaled back.

And please know that the things that are wasting your time aren't always bad things, but they aren't always the best things at this time. Sewing was not a "bad" thing, but I wasn't controlling it and the good that came from it was tainted by the havoc it was causing in my household. I had to let it go for a season. (I'm still letting it go, actually. Someday I hope to pick it back up, but for now, it is something I do not have time for.)

When you find your time wasters, ask the Lord for the courage and perseverance to let those things go. Have you family hold you accountable. Listen to the Lord's leading. It will bring the

CHAPTER 3

blessing of the time you need, even though it may be painful in the beginning.

Family first
We have a rule of thumb in this house:

If it doesn't benefit the family, it's not worth doing.

That means if one or more of us participates in an activity that begins to show signs of tearing away at the family's infrastructure, it needs to go…sooner, rather than later. In fact, it is best to assess an activity prior to participation because it is much harder to walk away from something once you've been involved in it for a while. Always remember, there will never be enough of you to go around if all you do is run around.

We also try to make the majority of our activities things the entire family can enjoy. This isn't possible in everything, but the more things you do as a family unit, the easier it is to meet everyone's needs as a mama.

Contentment is Key
Perhaps you think there isn't enough of you to go around because your children don't have the best of everything, the perfect day, their heart's desire every single moment of their little lives. Giving your children everything they want all the time will not build the strength of character they will need to be leaders in this world. They must understand through experience that the world does not revolve around them.

Enough of You to Go Around?

I am one person, and there are moments during the day when I have to choose one child over another. Not out of favoritism, but because wiping a little one's bum is more necessary than sharpening another one's pencil. I do my children a disservice if I try to pretend I'm some superwoman, there to do their bidding all day long. Patience, deference, humility and the likes are born out of hardship. Not that I want my children to have a hard life, but I shouldn't want them to have an easy life either.

You must also be content with your circumstances. If you are forever feeling discontent, you will never truly LIVE. If you are resentful of your life as a large family mama, your children and subsequently, everyone you come in contact with, will see only a harried, discontent, even angry woman instead of a woman depending on Christ for her every need. Everyone faces difficult circumstances in this life. How you face those situations is a true test of your character.

Relax
Savor that cup of tea, breathe that fresh air, smile more. Take naps with the kids, build forts out of blankets, have a conversation with a 5 year old.

If you are feeling worn thin then you probably are. God wants you to rest. He expects you to be still on occasion.

He created you. He gave you these children. He's not surprised by your circumstances or how busy your day is.

CHAPTER 3

Let Him lead. Let Him order your day. Lean on Him and know He will provide. He called you to this. He will equip you for this.

CHAPTER 4

Heart Schooling: The Art of Mothering

CHAPTER 4

Proverbs 1:8 says, *"Forsake not your mother's teaching."*

Even if you had not chosen to homeschool your large family, you would still be teaching them. By choosing to homeschool, you are purposefully and consciously stepping into the role of educator every day. But all too often homeschooling mothers step into their educator shoes and out of their mommy shoes, and next thing they know, they are living burdened and overwhelmed lives, devoid of anything that resembles enjoying their children. They wake up one morning and wonder if they would be a better mom if their kids just went to traditional school.

Homeschooling was never meant to be the burden we often make it. It was meant to be a way to teach, disciple, and live the Bible out moment by moment with our family. It was an opportunity to educate our children, guiding them gently toward Truth, grace, mercy, and love. It was a chance to teach them about the Lord and all His ways. It was to be a time of awe and wonder, growth and maturity. It was being there for the moments in life that count.

What happened between ideology and reality?

You quit being a mother.

There is something different about a mother's teaching. When we think about a mother's teaching, our minds immediately default to visions of grace and gentleness. We envision a mother gently guiding and instructing her child. It never looks

Heart Schooling: The Art of Mothering

like a crazy woman, frantically trying to push through the schoolwork before collapsing at the end of the day. And the Bible backs up the idea of a mother's teaching being beautiful:

"for they are graceful garlands for your head and pendants for your neck."
Proverbs 1:9

This verse inspires me. I want my teaching to be graceful. I want it to be something my children carry with them. I want it to be beautiful. The words of this verse do not sound like a burden. They sound amazing!

Today, I want to encourage you to set that homeschooling burden down, and instead, gather your children on your lap and be Mother. Be soft. Be gentle. Be grace-filled. Teach as a Mother, not a teacher. This is an opportunity of a lifetime! Make it beautiful!

Now, let's get practical...

What does Heart Schooling look like?

It's going to look a lot like life. It's going to look a lot like family. It may feel strange at first, but you will get the hang of it, I promise!

CHAPTER 4

> *{Note from Amy - Homeschooling Methods}*
> *There are a lot of homeschooling methods that lend themselves well to the "heart schooling" concept, but DO NOT lend themselves well to large families if you try to follow them to the tee. In the Appendix of this book, I will give you some ideas on how to tweak these methods to make them work with your particular family dynamic without feeling like a harried homeschool mom at the end of the day.*

First and foremost in this concept of Heart Schooling is God's Word. Scripture should permeate every aspect of your day. Your day starts there, your day ends there, your day is steeped in the Lord's precepts, principles and love.

Let me be quite clear...no curriculum can do this for you.

You are not going to find the magic-bullet curriculum that will teach your children the principles of God's Word for you. Nor will you find the perfect curriculum that will eliminate all your stressors and multi-level learning issues. There are great learning tools out there, but do not for one second believe the perfect one exists.

And do not for one second believe you will be able to be the perfect homeschool mom either. We are people and people make mistakes. God does not. Your children need to know you need God because you are imperfect! They need to know you make mistakes and God rights your wrongs. They need to know you do not expect perfection from them because we can only be

Heart Schooling: The Art of Mothering

made perfect in and through the person of Christ. Give them God...over and over and over again!

Start your Heart Schooling with your own relationship with Christ!
Your relationship with Christ must be evident to your children. Your children need to hear you speak of Him and His precepts in everything you do. They need to see you digging into the Word. They need to see you drinking the Living Water. Don't hide your faith. Offer praise where praise is due. Let your children see you come before the Throne with supplication for them, your homeschool, your entire life and the lives of others.

Start your day in the Word - not another "academic" subject.
Gather everyone in the living room and read the Bible first thing! Relate all other subjects back to His glory. Again, don't rely on the curriculum to do this for you (although there are some really good companies that produce materials that will help you facilitate this type of discussion.) You do not need to have only "religious" materials in your homeschool, but you DO need to present everything to your children through a Christian worldview. They need to understand how everything is inter-related and how God is Lord of all.

Emphasize discipleship.
By homeschooling your children, you are leading them. Be perfectly clear in WHERE you are leading them. You are either leading them toward the Lord or away from Him. This is the essence of discipleship - leading your child's heart and mind. "Fear of the Lord is the beginning of knowledge," and without

CHAPTER 4

Him, all else is simply information that "puffs up." In the end, it will not matter how smart your children appear to the world if their relationship with Christ is nonexistent.

Avoid textbooks {if you can}
Textbooks can be useful, especially for the large family mom who needs to spread her time between several children of several different levels and abilities. However, they tend to create a stilted atmosphere within the home, and more often than not, fail to encourage a child to dig deeper and look for ways to implement what they are learning into their own lives. They never truly "own" the information that comes from textbooks. I do use textbooks for math and grammar, but I try to encourage them to take what they are learning from those books and apply them outside of "school hours".

Dialogue, Dialogue, Dialogue
This is so important I said it 3 times! There is never a want for noise in a large family household, but don't let all that noise be the clanging of cymbals! We should be spending a goodly amount of our day conversing with our children because it is imperative they learn to apply knowledge to the world around them and it is your job to facilitate this discovery. You are a wealth of information for them simply because you are older and have lived more years. You are also their filter and sounding board for most of their growing up years. Things they encounter need your guiding hand and wisdom.

To keep a running dialogue with your children during the day will

Heart Schooling: The Art of Mothering

take conscious, purposeful parenting. It may even take setting aside time just for discussing things. No matter what it ends up looking like, the bottom line is be engaged!

Teach a love of learning by leading then letting go
Another aspect of Heart Schooling is giving your children a love of learning. Facilitate as many real-life learning opportunities as you can. This doesn't have to be museums and concerts. I know how difficult it can be to get out and about with a crew of small children, no matter how many big helpers you have. We live in an age when nearly everything you could possibly want to know is right at your fingertips! Turn on your computer and search out learning opportunities online. Watch orchestras and point out the instruments. Search out the name of the insect they found on their bedroom window. Be excited about learning new things and be excited for them as they learn new things!

From there, begin to show them HOW to learn on their own. Give them reference materials, take them to the library and show them how to use the internet {safely}. Slowly begin to let them explore on their own. Let them seek and search.

A good way to do this is to have them start searching things in the Bible. When they have a question or a character issue, point them toward God's Word. Perhaps they are having an issue with a friend or sibling. Ask them to research in the Bible what the answer to this issue might be. (It is important to have a good concordance available!) Scripture does not return void. You will see fruit from leading them to love learning from the Bible.

CHAPTER 4

Having their learning based in Scripture will give them a solid filter and foundation with which to strike out on their own and learn from other sources without being swayed by those opportunities. You will be able to let them go, trusting the Lord will guide their paths.

Encourage a heart for others
I tell my children I want them to learn to live open-handed. We are to love and know God so that we can love others. Being born into a large family naturally gives many opportunities to practice this.

However, I do not want to FORCE my children to love others. When someone is forced to "love" someone in actions or deeds, that love typically ends up fake and resented. We can encourage a heart for others, but we should never require it.

As with everything in our children's lives, we are training toward genuineness. We want their relationship with the Lord to be genuine and their relationship with others to also be genuine. Start in your own home by cultivating relationships that respect the individuality of each family member while teaching that individual gifts are blessings from the Lord in order that we might bless others.

I hope you are starting to catch a vision for the heart of your homeschool; however, before we conclude this chapter I want to say one thing...
I know you are tired.

Heart Schooling: The Art of Mothering

You are only 4 chapters into this book and you may already be overwhelmed. Thus far, we've talked a lot about foundations, but I know you purchased this book hoping to find practical help for surviving your large family homeschooling years.

The truth of the matter is, I can offer all the practical advice in the world, but you WILL fail. Homeschooling moms have a unique perspective of what it is like to fully and totally depend on God to get through the day. I'd encourage you to embrace this grace.

CHAPTER 4

A Large Family Homeschooling Mother's Prayer

Dear Lord,
I am tired, but You lift me up.
I am confused, but You make my paths straight.
I am busy, but You teach me to be still.
I am unsure, but You teach me to stand.
I am weary, but You give me life.
I am nothing, but You are my All.
May I declare to my children Your sufficiency
all day long.
Amen.

The Practical Stuff

CHAPTER 5

Herding Cats: How to Combat the Chaos

Herding Cats: How to Combat the Chaos

My husband likes to tell people that having a large family is like herding cats. In fact, as I'm typing this, my baby is scooting around in his walker, my 3 year old is taking a nap, my 5 and 8 year olds are making peanut butter and jelly sandwiches, my 9 year old is playing Minecraft, my 13 year old is copying recipes from a magazine, and my 16 year old is talking to me about computers. Tis a normal day here. 7 kids going in 7 directions.

Every child is unique and homeschooling a large group of children with varying interests and aptitudes can look a lot like herding cats. So, while I totally respect the "cat", I also know for sanity's sake, I need to at least attempt to orchestrate the chaos (and make peace with it at the same time!).

Have a Daily Routine or Schedule (or get one!)
There, I said it. You knew it was coming. We need to get this one out of the way right off the bat. (Sorry)

One of the first things you can do to make your homeschool and your life less chaotic is to adopt a daily rhythm to your life that incorporates all the things you need to get done in a day.

In my ebook, "The Homemaker's Guide to Creating the Perfect Schedule", I talk about the difference between a Scheduled Family and a Routine Family. It is so important to have a clear idea of how your family runs naturally, so you can harness that and focus it into something that works FOR you rather than AGAINST you.

CHAPTER 5

But remember, lists and charts and plans only work when you can implement them. Sometimes the lack of implementing a plan is laziness and sometimes it is simply the wrong plan. So, be diligent about finding something that works and trying it for a week or two before deciding if it needs a little tweaking or a toss out the window.

This is probably a good place to mention the fact that large families are forever in a state of change. While we'll talk more about specifics of these changes in other chapters, let's talk how they relate to our schedules right here, right now.

We can work hard to create the "perfect schedule", but more than likely, a few months down the road that schedule will need to change again. We have to stay flexible to those changes.

One really great way I have found to keep an adaptable schedule is to make what I call an At-A-Glance Schedule. This is a schedule that is specifically for Mommy.

The children are not the driving force behind your day – you are. Think about it for a moment…who in your home actually needs the schedule? 90% of the time, it is mom, and only mom, needing the schedule {in a household with only littles, this percentage jumps to 99.9%}. Instead of a schedule lining out everyone's day, most moms need one that orchestrates her day.

Herding Cats: How to Combat the Chaos

An example of an At-A-Glance Schedule follows:
8 am – Morning Chores, Quiet Time, Make Breakfast
9 am – BREAKFAST, Table Chores, 15 minute Tidy
9:30 am – Family Devotions
10 am – SCHOOL STARTS
11 am – Mom works with Middles & Littles, Bigs work independently
11:30 am – Lunch Prep
12 pm – LUNCH, Table Chores, 15 minute Tidy
1 pm – Mom works with Bigs
Middles/Littles – Pre-planned Activity
2 pm – Rest Time
3 pm – Special School
(activities like art and trips to the library)
4 pm – Projects / Outside Time
5 pm – Dinner Prep
6 pm – DINNER, Table Chores, 15 minute Tidy
7 pm – Free Time
8 pm – Jammies & Night Chores
8:30 pm – Family Devotions
9 pm – Bedtime
Mommy & Daddy Time

I have 2 copies of my At-A-Glance schedule printed and laminated, with one by my chair where most of the schooling takes place and the other hanging on the refrigerator. I can easily grab a glance and see exactly where my day is supposed to be.

CHAPTER 5

The best thing about this type of schedule is that it does not micromanage. My older children have their own routines that fit into the slots I've allowed for. I have not scheduled out their day for them because they are old enough to know what they need to get accomplished and how to go about accomplishing it. This is my schedule and it respects their schedule. You may not be to this place in your homeschooling, but someday you will have big kids…I promise. This type of schedule will carry you through from a house full of little ones to a house full of multiple ages to a house full of bigs quite nicely.

As you prepare to make a workable schedule for your household, do look at what other large families are doing. Ask those you know in real life, and take a look at some large family blogs.

Do remember that no two families are alike and you will not be able to entirely implement anyone else's schedule. I spent many years trying to be exactly like the other large families I knew and failed miserably because we weren't them and our circumstances were very different. Glean what you can from other large families and then make it your own.

OK, now that we have hashed out this schedule thing, we can move on. The next thing I want to talk about goes hand in hand with finding a schedule…

Plan when you can
There is a vicious cycle that can occur in a large homeschooling family:

Herding Cats: How to Combat the Chaos

lack of planning = crazy days
crazy days = lack of planning

You know you need to plan your school day/week/year so things will run smoothly, but you are so busy running your large family, you can't find the time to plan. (Ask me how I know.) That's why it is crucial you plan when you can.

I do a big overview planning of my school year in the early summer, but I plan specifics every weekend (except when this isn't feasible...more on that in a moment).

I look forward to my weekly homeschool planning sessions. Coffee in hand, books all over the place, and a feeling that I am actually accomplishing something is a very happy day for me. But, not always can I manage my weekend planning session. Sometimes the weekend is just too busy or we are out of town, or some other project needs me. Yet, I know if I don't plan, I won't get much accomplished and the whole family will feel like it is dissolving into chaos. (Remember in Chapter 3, I quoted Dwight D. Eisenhower? Raising a large family is not much different from commanding an army or running a country!)

Because planning is so important, I know I have to do it, but I can hear you now...
What if I can't find the time to do a major planning session yearly, monthly, or even weekly?

Never fear! While I highly encourage you to do your best to at

CHAPTER 5

least loosely plan a week at a time, if you are in a season (as if often the case for large families) of not being able to find the time to make broader plans, you can still have a successful and organized homeschool day.

First thing in the morning, grab a pen and paper and make a big list of everything you would like to accomplish that day in your homeschool. You may not get everything on that list done, but at least you planned it. (Remember the Eisenhower quote!)

Since we are going to dig deep into large family homeschool planning in Chapter 13, I'll leave off discussing planning to move on to a very important way to help curb the chaos in your homeschool...

Get a crew of vikings.
Oh, how I wish I could have seen your face just now as you read that! Allow me to elaborate... Years ago, I heard Gregg Harris give a session at a homeschool conference entitled Row Yourself to the Battle. Vikings never had slaves row them to their next battle, they always did it themselves, and if one viking didn't do his job, they all paid the price. We brought that concept into our home and homeschool by giving our children a meaningful part to play in the family. Everyone has a job. Every job is needed. Everyone in the family rows, we row together, and if someone is left rowing all by themselves with a project, you will often hear,

"Where are the rest of the vikings?!"

Herding Cats: How to Combat the Chaos

Let's look at some specifics as to how this works in a large family homeschool setting:
- Sometimes an older child will need to cook lunch or change a diaper.
- Sometimes a younger child will need to be given independent work.
- Sometimes a family project will take precedence over a personal projects.
- Sometimes we put off school for the day to get the "ship" back in order.

No matter what the specifics are, we are in this together, rowing together in the same direction!

Now is the time to foster a sense of family. Go back and read the chapter on Heart Schooling if need be. Understand what it means to love your children, love your husband, and listen to the Lord for guidance. Don't let the world dictate what a typical teenager acts like or how sibling relationships play out. What saith the Lord?

Families are important to the Lord. Start rowing!

Now that we have some vision to guide us out of chaos, let's talk a bit about some things that cause momentary detours. Up first, discipline issues! My best piece of advice here is:

Discipline with purpose.
We've all done it. At some point in our parenting we have dealt

CHAPTER 5

out a punishment that either didn't fit the crime or made absolutely no sense at all. Despite mistakes, we should all try to be purposeful in how we discipline. We should strive to make our disciplining biblical and relevant. It should never be random, and it should always be grace-filled.

Visit the Large Family Homeschooling Resource Webpage for a list of resources our family uses to aid us in this pursuit. Look under the listing for Chapter 5.
https://www.raisingarrows.net/lfhresources

The little ones
The youngest family members have a knack for creating detours, so much so that I dedicated entire chapters in this book to them. Your babies and toddlers are an important part of your day, and without a plan for them, you will either spend all day putting out fires or all day playing. If you need to head to those chapters right now, you are excused.

Last, but not least in this discussion on the handling of chaos in a large family homeshcool, is a topic that might cut a little deep.

Free yourself from distractions!
You might already know what I am going to say here, but it is important you hear me out and consider what aspects of this discussion can be applied to your particular brand of chaos. For the homeschooling mother, I believe the types of distractions she can control (to an extent) fall into what I call **Brain Clutter and Eye Clutter.**

Herding Cats: How to Combat the Chaos

Brain Clutter

Let me give you a personal example: The computer is my main researching tool and it keeps my always-thinking brain quite happy with information overload. But, this is not a good thing when I should be teaching school. It is important that I put limitations on my computer time to avoid being distracted away from the homeschooling at hand.

Brain Clutter would be anything that has your brain occupied away from the task at hand. If you are homeschooling, you should not be menu planning or pinning things on Pinterest, or even reading a book on homeschooling.

If you feel yourself being pulled toward these things, it would be a good idea to do a "brain dump" where you get everything that is in your head out on a piece of paper and come back to it when you are finished with the homeschooling lessons.

Perhaps you need to set limitations like "no computer time until after school is finished" or "no school on menu planning days". Only you know what kind of Brain Clutter you deal with and what it will take to solve it. It might be drastic, and it might hurt at first, but, in the end your homeschool will thank you!

Eye Clutter

Another example from my own life:

A messy home makes homeschooling difficult for me. When my children were 12 and under, we got up every morning and

CHAPTER 5

did cleaning chores before school hours. The simple fact of the matter was that in order to be productive, my home needed to be clean. Looking back, I wish I had learned the lesson of going to bed with a clean home. That would have made my eye clutter a lot less!

And finally, the best way to herd those cats is to

Stay calm
This may sound trite, but if mama is calm, life is more manageable. You have to practice being calm. You have to have the wherewithal to step outside yourself in the middle of the storm and see the situation for what it is. These little ones weren't put on this earth to stress you out. They are not trying to undo you. They are children...plain and simple. They have not learned to curb their selfishness. They need grace, mercy and guidance from a mother who is calm enough to realize all of this.

Trust me, you can have a large AND peaceful household, but peace radiates from within. Let the Lord fill you up to overflowing. And when you feel empty, pray through it.

CHAPTER 6

Keeping It Clean

CHAPTER 6

I used to think it was utterly impossible to homeschool AND keep a clean house. I figured I was giving up a clean home when I decided to homeschool because there simply were not enough hours in the day to do both, and I knew plenty of other homeschool moms who would back me up on my theory.

Yet, I never, ever felt comfortable having a messy home, and our homeschooling never, ever felt right as long as the house was in disarray. Deep within me I knew I had to find a way to keep the house tidy while homeschooling.

Before I go any further into this whole cleaning business, I want to make it clear that **the purpose of a home is not to create a place that sacrifices the family on the altar of appearances.** (Read that again.)

Moving on…

Every home is unique, so what has worked for me won't necessarily work for you, but I do want to give you some suggestions and tools to help you find what works for you, but ultimately, it will be up to you to implement them and adjust them.

Let's break things down by family stages: All Littles, A Mix of Bigs & Littles, and All Bigs.

"Help, I only have littles!"
There are days when all you do is put out fires. You might even wonder why you would bother cleaning anything when the

Keeping It Clean

moment you turn around, it will all explode again.

Little people are notorious mess makers. They don't have much of a concept of how to clean up after themselves, so they often resemble the Tasmanian devil on the Saturday morning cartoons. When you have only littles, you are the primary cleaner-upper, but you know full well, cleaning up after a large family by yourself is nearly impossible. Time to delegate...to yourself! That's right! You CAN delegate chores to yourself in manageable pieces that will help you get everything done with the least amount of stress.

Here's how:

1. Write down every REAL chore that needs to be done in your home. Don't be crazy with this list. In other words, you could write down "wipe down baseboards" or "clean ceiling", but those are NOT necessary to the functioning of your home. They are extras and can be saved for once or twice a year or as you have a moment of extra time.

The chores you write down may look something like this:
Sweep & Mop Floors
Vacuum Carpets
Dust
Tidy Bedrooms
Pick Up Toys
Do Dishes

2. Divide your list by what must be done daily ("must" being

CHAPTER 6

the key word here) and what can be done weekly and still be ok. Again, don't be crazy. You DO NOT have to mop your floor every day. I know you might WANT to, but when you have all littles, mopping really good once a week and spot mopping as needed is perfectly acceptable.

3. Divide up your weekly chores by day of the week. When I had only littles, this is what my Weekly Chore List looked like:
Monday: Dust
Tuesday: Sweep & Mop & Vacuum
Wednesday: Clean Bedroom & Bathroom
Thursday: Office Day
Friday: Errand Day/Shopping Day
Saturday: Outside Chores
Sunday: Rest

I enlisted my little helpers to "help", but I did most of the work. I did all of this AFTER breakfast and BEFORE school hours. It took about an hour to accomplish. Was my house clean all at one time? Not often. But, I knew every week each essential area would get cleaned.

4. Carve out small slots of time to get the daily chores accomplished. In the morning, after every meal, in the afternoon, right before bed...these are all good times to take 15 minutes to do as many of the daily chores as you can.

Keeping It Clean

> *{Note from Amy - Getting it ALL Clean}*
> *There are times when a home needs to be all clean. There are also those of you with husbands who prefer the entire home be fully clean every day. The method above is not a method for getting it ALL clean at one time. That requires a chunk of time devoted to cleaning.*
>
> *When you have only littles and need to get the entire house clean, you will have to carve out time (preferably toward the end of your day) when you can lay children down for naps or segregate them in a safe place and take focused time to clean.*
>
> *When you need to marathon clean, get focused and work with purpose. Start in one room/area, get it done without moving on. I will often go room by room, piling things at the door or in a basket (which can be handed to a child to be put away or at the very least, put in the proper room). Once a room is finished I turn off the light and shut the door (if possible). This tells me and the children that that room is finished.*

Bigs & Littles

This is the place in life most large homeschooling families find themselves in most often -- a mix of bigs and littles. "Bigs" is also a very relative term. At one point in time my bigs were 10 and 7. My current 7 year old is a "middle" in my eyes, not a big, but that's because the "bigs" just kept getting bigger!

CHAPTER 6

You know you have "bigs" when they start being truly helpful with cleaning chores. In the Appendix of this book, you will find a list of Age-Appropriate Chores, but remember, just because a chore is "age-appropriate" does not mean your child will do the job at the same level you would do the same chore. Even "bigs" don't always manage to do a chore fully and completely. You will need to check and recheck, doing your best to liberally hand out grace and mercy.

Two years ago, I came to a place where I had at least one child who was a full-fledged big. He could do work that was complete and efficient. He was 13. It was then I decided to move away from a weekly chore list to a One Day Home Blessing. For us, this was a wonderful thing, but you may find you need to stay in the weekly chore list for a long time or even find a different way to make your chores effective.

The reason the Home Blessing worked so well for us was because I had children capable of working independently so the house could be cleaned top to bottom in record time (about 2 hours). During that time, my littles would do their chores and then play in one room while the rest of us finished our chores. I did my chores and kept an eye on everyone else's chores to make sure the work was being done completely. The reward for all their hard work was no school that day and time for movies and games after their chores were complete.

Another great method for a mix of bigs and littles are charts with chores listed on them. Divide up your chores amongst the

Keeping It Clean

children and then make out checklists for them to work through every day. For your non-readers, use pictures and explain what those pictures mean.

You can make these chores required before school or before play in the afternoon after school. Consider when your children do their best work and what motivates them, and adjust accordingly.

Only Bigs
Having only bigs presents challenges all their own. You would think this would be an easy time, but it isn't because children who are now big tend to have bigger schedules as well. They do keep a house cleaner, but when you really need to crack down and clean, they may not be there due to jobs, outside activities or school work.

One way to approach cleaning chores with only bigs is to give them jurisdictions within the home that are their domain to take care of while encouraging them to pick up after themselves.

A One Day Home Blessing works well too, but keep in mind their individual schedules. When can you schedule something like this that will have everyone at home at the same time? How can you handle things if one member of the family is out? You will have to adjust and adapt often, and eventually, you will find yourself back to doing many of the chores on your own again as your children leave the home one by one. Thankfully, as they leave, they tend to take their messes with them, unlike when they were small children.

CHAPTER 6

> *{Note from Amy - A Word of Caution About Bigs}*
> *Many parents feel sorry for their older children who now have bigger schedules. They will make concessions that become the norm. For instance, a child has a big exam to study for so a parent does their kitchen chores, only to find that child seems to ALWAYS have something "big" to do.*
>
> *While it is perfectly acceptable to help your child out by taking their chores upon yourself from time to time, it is never ok for a child*
> *living in your home to not contribute to the home - this includes adult children.*
>
> *You are doing your child a disservice if you do not require them to help in the running of the home. Their chores won't necessarily be what they were when they were 12, but you need to see your home as a place where everyone has a part to play that contributes to the orderliness of the home. Your child will experience this in their place of business and their own home someday. Teach them this responsibility now.*

The Bottom Line
You are both wife and mother. You are both homeschool mom and homemaker. This is not mission impossible. You can keep a clean home and homeschool at the same time. You may struggle with perfectionism or laziness or distractions, but those cannot become excuses.

Keeping It Clean

Ask God to point out where you need to focus your energies in order to have the house cleaned to His standards. Ask God to show you where you are expecting too much or expecting too little. Ask God to show you the proper order for your day.

Listen and then do.
You don't have to be perfect, but you do need to be obedient.
God will honor your efforts

CHAPTER 7

Organizing the Large Family Homeschool

Organizing the Large Family Homeschool

I love the concept of cutesy color-coordinated, unbelievably streamlined, beautifully labeled organizing, but putting it into practice is too time consuming for my liking. The large family mom needs quick and simple homeschool organizational methods that will work for the large family household without a lot of fuss. So, here you go...

Bookshelves
I have yet to meet a homeschooling mother who doesn't like bookshelves. They are an absolute necessity in a large family household! Following are a few ideas you can mix and match to make your bookshelves more organized and user-friendly.

1. Main Bookshelves
For a long time these were my only bookshelves. They were (and still are) a hodgepodge of bookshelves I picked up along the way at auctions, discount stores, and from friends and family. My attempts to make them pretty have proven futile, but pretty doesn't help the functionality.

What you have is what you have - make it work!

When your children are younger or your house is smaller, main bookshelves may be all you need. Keep them in a centralized location and organize by sections.

Years ago, I had a friend help me sort out all my books by kind and then we labeled the sections with hand-written paper labels covered over with clear packing tape. Some of the sections we

CHAPTER 7

had were Biographies, Science, Youth Fiction, Baby, History, etc.

Now, our main bookshelves are kept in the family room and hold only the books that are not separated out into other areas. When possible, I prefer segregating books using a variety of the methods below.

Separate by owner -
I use the term "owner" loosely, because we all know that books may have multiple owners and are more often than not, handed down from child to child. Books that are mainly used by your girls go in their room in a bookshelf, crate or basket. Books mainly used by the boys go in their room. Family books go in the family room on the main bookshelves. Mom and Dad's books go in their room. Baby's books go on a lower shelf in the family room or in a basket for easy access.

Separate by location -
In my opinion, nearly every room in the house should have a bookshelf! This method of organizing attests to that. Kitchen books/cookbooks go in a bookshelf near the kitchen (or in a cupboard if you can spare one), school books go in the school room, computer and technology books go near the computer or office space, etc. Consider where you will use a book the most and put it there!

Separate by kind -
I like to go through all our homeschool books at the beginning of every school year and separate them by kind. This creates

Organizing the Large Family Homeschool

several categories that will then need to be organized into bookshelves and other storage areas.

For instance, I keep all the Science books and curriculum aids for the year in one place so that no one has to scramble to find exactly what they need. The text books, test forms, experiments, microscope and slides, notebooks, and workbooks are all together.

Likewise, the Five in a Row books and notebooks are all in the same place along with things I need for corresponding crafts and deeper study. It makes my life easier to have things separated this way.

The Books of the Year Bookshelf
We keep a bookshelf near our dining room that houses all the living books that will be used during the current school year. This keeps everything for the year in one place so I don't spend precious time hunting down that one book we need to finish our Ancient Egypt study. This has been a huge time-saver and probably ranks right up there as one of my favorite homeschool organizational tips.

Corporate Studies Bookshelf
When I use the word "corporate" I mean anything we do together as a family during our homeschool day. The corporate bookshelf is home to our Bibles, our devotionals, the read-aloud history books I have all the children listen to (pulled from the Books of the Year Bookshelf), our art DVDs,

CHAPTER 7

and various audios and DVDs that go along with our school work.

The Homeschool Closet
I have had some type of homeschool closet since the very beginning of my homeschooling years. When I can spare the space, I like to use a literal closet with shelves. I have also used a cheapie-stand-alone storage closet with doors. Anything with doors can become a Homeschool Closet.

I consider the Homeschool Closet to be one of the essentials of homeschooling organization. Homeschool books are not used every year, even when you have back to back to back children. You have to have a way to store all the unused curriculum.

This is also a good place to put those items you use only occasionally that would be in the way if left out. This is a great place for scratch paper, crayons and other art supplies, media and manipulatives.

Mom's Basket
Individualized Mom baskets are a great organizational tool. I keep a Nursing Basket in the newborn days with everything I need at hand. I keep a Diapering Basket in my bedroom for easy diaper changes.

The Homeschool Mom's Basket is similar in concept. This is the basket of curriculum and extras you need easy access to. The things in this basket are used nearly every day and are often pulled from the Corporate Studies Bookshelf. Items that

Organizing the Large Family Homeschool

might be in this basket include pens and scratch paper, your current read aloud, your iPad or tablet, your Bible.

Keep your Mom's Basket in the place you are most likely to be while homeschooling. I keep mine beside my chair in the living room. Much of our schooling takes place in the living room. My basket makes a handy place to put everything I need so all I have to do is reach down and grab the next thing.

School Binder {or similar method} for Mom
Until recently, I kept a school binder for myself. It had schedules and ideas, extra notebook paper, and odds and ends I found myself referring to on occasion. This year, I went to a digital system using Evernote (a free online service) as my main "binder".

I like the paperless system, but it is not for everyone. The idea here is to create a "catch-all" for yourself. If you can use your Mom's Basket for this purpose, that's great too. Whatever method you use, this is to act as your "brain" and catch and hold everything you need to make your day run smoothly.

Library Bag/Box
Take a large family to a library and you will soon see WHY you need a place specifically for your library books. Even with our 3 books per child rule, we end up with a massive collection of books that need to be kept separate from our own personal library.

CHAPTER 7

We have used a large utility tote from ThirtyOne Gifts that was nice for transporting the books to and from the library. We have also used a plastic tub with handles that keeps the books neat and tidy at home.

You will need to encourage your children to return the library books to their box, and be sure to sign up for email notices so you know when to return or recheck books.

Bible Box
Growing weary of scrambling every Sunday to gather Bibles for church, we decided to create a Bible Box. This is the same concept as the Library Box - a place to keep your Bibles from getting lost or torn up.

My older children tend to keep track of their own Bibles, but the younger ones need a place to keep their Bibles safe. Any basket, box, or bag will work, just be sure to keep it handy and easily accessible!

Organizing Extras
Homeschooling naturally creates a lot of extra things that must be organized. Everything from paper and pencils to art supplies to DVDs and CDs need to find a home. Take some time to jot down what needs to be organized in your homeschool, and then see which of the following organizers fit your needs best.

Plastic totes and containers
If it needs to be organized, then chances are there is a plastic

Organizing the Large Family Homeschool

tote or container made just the right size and shape!

Metal containers
Despite metal's industrial look, you can pull off some very fun (and durable) organization with metal containers. Don't be afraid to paint them either!

Baskets
Oh, how I love baskets! They make the ugliest of things look lovely. Add a bit of fabric for a more decorative/designer look!

Binders & Page protectors
I love the versatility of binders and page protectors. Everything from ebooks to nature notebooks can be put in binders. I actually keep a stash of binders, page protectors, and notebook tabs on hand because I never know when I might need them!

Laminator
For a large family, it is imperative you take as many measures as you can to make things last. A laminator helps with that. Amazon runs specials on the laminator I use a couple of times a year or you can buy it at your local superstore for a little better price than Amazon's every day price.

We laminate things like schedules, chore lists, things we've cut from newspapers or magazines that need to be kept and referenced.

CHAPTER 7

Keepy app
You can't keep everything.

While "Homeschool Mom Of Two" can keep all sorts of papers and drawings, and awards, "Homeschool Mom of Many" cannot. It would be a logistical nightmare.

Enter Keepy! This has got to be one of the funnest apps I have on my iPad! I uploaded each of my children's names, stats and photos and then whenever I have something of theirs that is super awesome or super cute that I would love to keep, but know I can't, I snap a photo and save it in Keepy.

You could do this with a regular camera and file them on your computer as well. Whatever you do, the idea is to save some things in digital form and throw away the hard copy.

External hard drive
Don't forget to keep your computer decluttered! I am so glad I finally decided to buy an external hard drive for our household. I use my hard drive to store all the computer files and photos that are not immediately needed on my computer. This is a great way to keep ebooks, old lesson plans, files you have downloaded and plan to use for school, but not this year.

For more organizing resources and articles, visit the Large Family Homeschooling Resource Page - https://www.raisingarrows.net/lfhsresources

CHAPTER 8

Getting Your Homeschool Day Started Off on the Right Foot

CHAPTER 8

Mornings have never been easy for me. I am naturally a night person. However, even as a certified night owl, I have realized that in order to be a good homeschool mom, I have to greet the morning with more than a grunt.

The large family mom has plenty of responsibilities to take care of every morning, but please do not neglect giving your day to God first and foremost.

While I do not believe that you must have your Quiet Time alone in the morning, I do believe without centering your day on Christ, you will head your day in the wrong direction.

In those seasons of motherhood where you have more leisure in the mornings, feel free to start your day with coffee and your Bible, planning and focusing your day. In the seasons when you must hit the ground running, pray through it and take your Quiet Time when and where you can get it.

{Note from Amy - The Proverbs 31 Woman}
She gets up while it is still dark; she provides food for her family and portions for her servant girls.
~Proverbs 31:15

This verse in Proverbs is often misunderstood. It is less about what time she gets up and more about why she gets up. She greets the morning with productivity rather than laziness. She gets up and takes care of her responsibilities. We need to be certain our morning routines reflect a conscious effort to take

Getting Your Homeschool Day Started Off on the Right Foot

> *care of our responsibilities in the name of our Lord, Jesus Christ.*

I do believe no matter how crazy your day may start, your homeschool day needs to start in the Word. Whether you gather everyone around the breakfast table or in the living room or school room, start your child's learning at the beginning of knowledge and wisdom - God's Word.

Our homeschool day starts in the living room with everyone grabbing their Bibles from the Bible Box {see Chapter 7} and turning to the passage for the day. Most of the time our morning devotionals consist of reading through a chapter a day of a single book in the Bible. However, we have done many different things over the years including following reading plans and working through devotionals I had purchased. The goal is to get your family in the Word and learn the habit of reading their Bibles.

After our Bible reading, we read from missionary books. My goal is to show my children God's Word in action. I want to give them food for thought as they step into their academic studies. I want them to realize that God's Word is living and breathing and is the center of everything they do. I feel missionary stories help to give them this focus.

Homeschooling a large family is hard work. Getting your homeschool day started with God will give you and your children the strength needed to keep going.

CHAPTER 8

Remember: "Whatever you do, work heartily, as for the Lord and not for men" ~Colossians 3:23

CHAPTER 9

Homeschooling from the Bottom to the Top

CHAPTER 9

When my older two children were first homeschooling and my other children were all too young for "real school", my homeschooling was pretty simple. I would set the littles to play or wait for their nap time and then start school, working between the two older children without much trouble. Even when I added a third child, I still managed to get it all done in this rather haphazard way. However, once I was homeschooling more than 3 children, I realized there was no way this was going to work...at least not very well. I also noticed I was no longer able to find the time to do the fun things with my younger crowd that I had done when my older children were their age. It was disheartening and I had to face some hard truths.

My little ones were being left behind.

As my olders grew, I grew with them, but I often forgot to step back down and be there for my littles. It was so easy to get caught up with all the neat things my older children were doing and learning, but equally easy to accidentally let the entire day slip by without doing a single lesson with my younger children. My little ones had absorbed a fair share of Latin, and they were listening in on read-alouds, but there was no focus and purpose to their learning. Without focused time and energy spent with them, they would simply drift along, never truly grasping concepts.

I needed a way to get it all done, efficiently, effectively and joyfully. One of the ways I did this was to school my littles first. Doing school with them first ensured they received my focused

Homeschooling from the Bottom to the Top

attention first thing while the older children worked on independent studies that did not require my help. Doing this one little thing completely turned our homeschool around!

Let me share with you a bit more in-depth about how this works: After our morning chores, we start our school day as I explained in the previous chapter. From there everyone breaks away to their independent studies. My older children get started with their work on their own. I get my middles started with math and handwriting while I sit down to do phonics with the newest reader-in-training. I also do some math work and sometimes some fun little activities as well. Once I've finished with the youngest school-age child, I move up the ladder to the middles and help them with any questions they have. From there, I like to gather the middles and youngers for some activities they can all do together *(more on that in the next chapter)*.

Usually I can get all of this accomplished by lunch time. After lunch, I work with the older kids on their corporate work or we do family projects (again, I'll talk more in-depth about this in the next chapter).

CHAPTER 9

> {Note from Amy - Do you have to school the littles every day?}
> The idea of homeschooling from the bottom to the top every day may feel overwhelming. Some days have more packed into them and sometimes the older children truly do need more of your time.
>
> If you cannot manage to school your littles every day, that is perfectly alright; however, consistency is important, and the only way you will achieve consistency is by doing school with your younger crowd on a regular basis.
>
> I'd encourage you to make a schedule at the beginning of each semester or life season that gives you a guide to work within. Here are a few ideas to make that work:
> - Do workbook subjects on Monday, Wednesday, and Friday and make Tuesday and Thursday "Fun Days".
> - Do phonics every day and math twice a week.
> - Do phonics two days in a row and fill in the other subjects on the other days.
> - School the littles every day but Friday.
>
> The possibilities are endless!

CHAPTER 10

Corporate Homeschooling

CHAPTER 10

Every large homeschooling family naturally looks for ways to make their day run smoother and more efficiently. Most everyone knows the more subjects and activities you can combine and include multiple ages in, the easier things will be, but being told to do this and actually knowing how to practically implement this concept are two very different things. This chapter will hopefully shine a light on how corporate homeschooling can work for your family.

Hang on tight - this is going to be one meaty chapter!

Corporate Homeschooling Model #1
The One-Room Schoolhouse Model

Have you ever been driving along and noticed an old country schoolhouse on the side of the road? I am fascinated by old schoolhouses. Perhaps it is because I grew up watching Little House on the Prairie or because my own father was schooled in a one-room schoolhouse in rural Kansas, but whenever we pass by one of these dilapidated old buildings, I stare and wonder at who might have gone to school there so many years ago, trudging through thick snow in black boots and prairie dresses, lunch pail in hand.

I now have my own one-room schoolhouse of sorts. No, we don't trudge through snow to get here or wear prairie dresses (except when we are pretending) or eat our lunch from pails (except when we are pretending), but I do teach in a way that is rather reminiscent of days gone by. This sort of homeschooling

Corporate Homeschooling

is a great way to get your feet wet with the concept of corporate homeschooling.

Here's how to get started:

Set up a close-knit learning environment
In the one-room schoolhouses of yesteryear, all ages of children were in close proximity to each other. Our family likes to gather in the living room and fill up all the seating and floor space. Sometimes the older children grab their laptops and meet at the dining room table with tons of discussion over where they are in a certain subject.

The idea here is to allow your children to be near each other as they learn. If you have children who need quiet and solitude to really learn their lessons, that is fine too, but when they are finished, encourage them to rejoin the family unit and overhear the other learning going on. Let them soak in the sounds of learning without the stress of expectations.

I'll talk more in a bit on how this close-knit environment facilitates learning.

Center your subjects on the Bible.
Before every bit of Christianity was removed from the public school system, the Bible was the book by which all things were judged and measured. While I do not believe the one-room schoolhouses executed this in a manner befitting of Deuteronomy 6 where the Israelites were exhorted to teach the

CHAPTER 10

Lord's ways to their children day and night and everywhere in between, I do believe the rural schools, like where my father attended, did acknowledge God as the ultimate authority.

So, let me encourage you take it much further than the one-room schoolhouse model ever took this concept.

Stick with me while we wade in deep...

You do not have to exclusively use Christian curriculum to homeschool your children with a Bible-centered education. However, you do need to know how to center your subjects from a Biblical worldview. You cannot simply place Christian materials in front of your children and think your job is over and they are somehow going to soak it all up and become a Christ follower via the cutely illustrated Bible stories they read every day.

Don't go searching out your next homeschool curriculum based on how well IT teaches your child about Christ, but rather how well you can USE it to disciple your children and how well it fits with what a real Christian education looks like.

Proverbs 4:11 says,
"I have taught you in the way of wisdom; I have led you in right paths."

This is a father speaking to his son, but in this chapter he also mentions the child's mother and her teachings as well. The

Corporate Homeschooling

point I want to make here is contained in these words...

I have taught

I have led

This is not someone else's job, and you would think as homeschoolers we would understand that. Unfortunately, all too often, we bring our babies home only to hand them over to that great Christian curriculum we bought at the homeschool convention.

We have to think bigger and dig deeper. We have to quit looking at the trees and start focusing on the forest. We have to lead our children in the right paths. We can't expect anyone or anything else to do it for us.

Seek the Lord in every subject you teach your children. How is God going to use that subject for His glory? How can you glorify Him through it? Some subjects will be easier to do this with, while some subjects will simply teach you and your child to persevere through trials! Go on a God-hunt and enjoy the journey!

Work from youngest to oldest
We already talked at length about this in the previous chapter, but let me reiterate this classic one-room schoolhouse paradigm. The younger children, whose attention spans were considerably shorter, had the teacher's focus at the beginning of class. In my early years of homeschooling multiple ages, I

CHAPTER 10

always set my school up with the intent that I would school the littles in the afternoon after all the bigs had finished their work. However, more often than not, I never got around to schooling the littles. Once I started making them the first thing on my list for the day, it was amazing how much we accomplished!

The Trickle-down effect
One room schoolhouses were conducive to exposing younger children to what they would be learning in upcoming years because of the close-knit learning environment I mentioned above. By the time the children were being taught in the upper levels, they had more than likely heard all the material several times.

The way we capture this in our homeschool is through something I call the trickle-down effect. I encourage the younger children to stay in the room and play quietly while I read to or have discussions with the older children. While they may not catch everything that is being said, I am always surprised by how attentive they are and how much they do manage to absorb.

Plan school around the needs of the family
Back in the one room schoolhouse days, the family was still in charge. School was secondary. If there was work on the farm, school could wait. If it was time for harvest, school let out. Don't let the school calendar rule you if there are opportunities to engage in as a family.

Corporate Homeschooling

Go outside
This may sound simplistic, but I often forget how much children need fresh air and exercise. The one-room schoolhouse was filled with children who not only walked to and from school, but also had a recess during school and chores afterward! For boys especially, this is a necessity to keep their little minds from wandering during class time.

Take meals together
One thing I love about homeschooling is that we are able to break bread as a family at least twice a day if not more. This is one area the one-room schoolhouse did not do as well as the family could. Meals are a great opportunity for learning, so don't forget how important this is!

Expect order
You didn't mess around with the one-room schoolhouse teacher. Raps on knuckles, spankings, and seats in corners were just a few of the punishments dolled out to children who did not keep the order. An orderly school day is a pleasure to all those involved, so don't be afraid to expect order and enforce it in a way that is meaningful and effective (in a more loving, motherly way, of course!).

Seek mastery
Years ago, the standard of the one room schoolhouse was the standard held by parents at home. That standard was mastery. Somewhere along the way, we lost the drive to master a subject and became complacent and willing to substitute "good

CHAPTER 10

enough" for "well done."

I have high expectations for my children. I am not wanting to make round pegs fit in square holes, nor frustrate my children, but I do expect them to do everything "as unto the Lord." We don't go by grade levels, we don't push through textbooks so we can get to the other side, and we don't consider a C to be average.

As I look through these points, perhaps it isn't the one room schoolhouse model I am truly after, but rather the Deuteronomy 6 schoolhouse I am after. For one room schoolhouses, despite my imaginations, were not perfect; however, Scripture always is. And maybe, just maybe, what the one room schoolhouse tried to do had already been done.

So, while I look to the one room schoolhouse as a model, it is not because I believe it was the epitome of proper education. It is simply because I believe the one room schoolhouse of yesteryear in rural Kansas can teach this public-schooled mama trying-to-make-her-way-as-a-homeschooler a thing or two. I'm sure you can see the merit in that.

Corporate Homeschooling Model #2
Combining Subjects and Ages

One of the most efficient ways to homeschool a large family is to combine subjects and ages as much as possible. Here are some guidelines for figuring out how to do this:

Corporate Homeschooling

List every subject for every child
Go ahead. I'll wait. Ok, now that you've done that...

Look to see where subjects overlap
Science below jr. high level and sometimes even high school level is easily combined. Teach from the same book - it's ok! Grammar can be taught corporately as well. History? Yes, indeed! Even spelling, literature, writing, foreign language and a whole host of other subjects can be taught corporately! Get creative and in the end, save yourself time and money!

Look for curriculum that encourages combining ages
We use Tapestry of Grace, but I know there are many others out there that are designed to be used with multiple ages. These types of curricula are not absolutely necessary, but they can be helpful in helping you know how to combine ages.

Corporate Homeschooling Model #3
Chain-Link Learning

While the trickle-down effect mentioned above acknowledges that younger children naturally pick up on what their older siblings are learning. Chain-link learning is more purposeful. This is the act of actually connecting the youngers with the olders to create a learning opportunity.

So, let me give you some practical application ideas so you can easily start doing this in your homeschool!

CHAPTER 10

Learn – Teach – Learn Chain-linking
This type of chain-linking focuses on teaching the older children something that can then be translated by them into a lesson for the younger children. For instance, when my older children were learning about Early American History, I had them put together a lapbook on Colonial America. But rather than completing the lapbook themselves, they helped their younger siblings complete the lapbook.

Another example would be how my high schooler does his science experiments and then gathers all the other children around to look through the microscope while he explains what he's been doing in science and what they are looking at through the lens.

The first example was something I put together. The second example just happened. The more you set up this kind of chain-linking, the more likely your children will find their own opportunities to follow the Learn-Teach-Learn example.

Buddy-Up Chain-linking
In my opinion, this kind of chain-linking should be kept to a minimum. On occasion, it is perfectly acceptable to have an older child team up with a younger child and actually teach a lesson or help out with a workbook. This gives the older child practice at leading and the younger child practice at learning from someone other than mom. Both have their advantages, but beware not to abuse this convenience. You are mom and they need you.

Corporate Homeschooling

Another way you can do this is to pair an older child with a younger child to share with each other from their lessons. They take turns sharing, giving each an opportunity to hone public speaking and listening skills, all the while learning from each other.

Plan – Participate Chain-linking
This kind of chain-linking is downright fun! This is what happens when you have an end-of-unit party or a field trip that goes with something you are learning. So for instance, when we finished our Medieval Time Period in history, we planned a Medieval Feast. We included things that could be done by both the older crowd and the younger crowd. The older children presented papers and the younger children did crafts. Everyone planned, everyone participated. Everyone had a blast!

Corporate Homeschooling Model #4
Life Learning

We are not a homeschooling family...we are a family who homeschools. If we are constantly trying to make our lives fit into the confines of a traditional school day, we will quite possibly miss out on some awesome opportunities that have value far beyond what a textbook can teach. Don't let school rule your family or ruin your family.

Your goal is to teach a love of learning and create life-long learners. Does your school day match that goal?

CHAPTER 10

Is your curriculum full of busy work? Learn to tweak it or ditch it! Does it take entirely too much time out of your day, leaving you very little time for deep and meaningful conversations with your children? Look for something that doesn't monopolize your life.

Living life and teaching life skills are so important. Seize those opportunities that take you outside the classroom. Teach your children to work hard and be responsible. Learn to see homeschooling as a lifestyle and not something you do in order to check off SCHOOL on your To-Do List.

So, what does this Life Learning look like and how do you know if you are actually doing "school"?

For the sake of those of you who need to keep track of school hours, let's break this down. Life skills count as school if they are being actively taught. So, if you are actively and purposefully teaching your children, it is school.

What do I mean by "actively taught?" If you use a life skill to teach formal school subjects, then you can count those hours as school hours. You must be engaging your children in conversation and education and they must be engaging in the act of learning. You cannot simply DO a life skill and then call it school, but you certainly can teach along with the life skill and call that school.

Here are some examples of life skills and the school subjects

Corporate Homeschooling

they might encompass:

Grocery shopping
- Math – price comparison, weights, units
- Nutrition – calories, ingredients, additives, preservatives
- Science – digestive tract, food production
- Geography – origin of foods

Doctor's office
- Science – anatomy, medicine
- Math – weights, measurements, volume

House cleaning
- Home economics
- Science – properties of common cleaners

Vacation
- History – points of interest, historical figures and events of area
- Math – mileage
- Geography – map reading, topography

Hunting & Shooting sports
- Science – animal science
- History – history of hunting and weapons
- Math – trajectory, distances, windage and elevation, reloading and ammunition
- Geography – landscape

CHAPTER 10

Sewing
- Math – measurements, angles
- Science – textiles, gears and machines
- History

Post Office
- Math – weights, money
- History

Dining out
- Math – money
- Nutrition – food groups, menus, content
- Foreign language – based on restaurant
- Cultural studies - decor, music, food

The possibilities truly are endless, but remember, you have to be actively and purposefully teaching while engaged in these life skills and activities in order to call it school. This is life learning and is very much something that can be done with the entire family.

Hopefully, you've gathered some ideas from this chapter for how to corporate homeschool your large family. It really is an exercise in creativity and perseverance as you put together something that works for your family. Keep after it! You will find your large family homeschooling groove!

CHAPTER 11

Chunk Learning

CHAPTER 11

If there is one thing the large family homeschooling mom finds herself short on, it would be time. More often than not, I wake up and next thing I know I'm getting ready for bed! Time races by and I hang on, white-knuckled.

When it comes to teaching all the subjects you want to get in during the course of a homeschool day, it is easy to see where time marches on despite your best efforts to get through all your lesson plans. This is why I highly recommend using the Chunk Learning approach.

The basic idea behind this concept is to take certain subjects in chunks of concentrated learning. There are a couple of ways you can implement this effectively in your large family homeschool.

Crash Course (Once and/or Repeated)
One subject we crash course is Grammar. I give my children some basic foundations for grammar throughout their elementary years, but in jr. high and high school, we do a once-a-week crash course and run pell-mell through grammar lessons, doing entire units in each session.

I reinforce what they are learning via essays and papers that correspond with other subjects, but I do not require grammar as an every day, every year subject.

Sometimes a crash course chunk learning session need only be a one-time deal. This would be in the instance of something

Chunk Learning

you feel a child may have missed or needs to relearn, but could easily catch up on in a quick one-on-one session.

Sometimes a crash course needs to be a regular thing as in the case of a subject that could be covered quicker and more efficiently with just a bit of concentrated effort once a week or even once a month.

A Focused Season
This was something suggested to us by a college counselor who understood homeschooling. It's been a little difficult for me to wrap my brain around, but if you are willing to think (and do) outside the box, then it won't be long before you'll see the merit in this way of chunk learning.

Rather than doing all subjects all year long, take subjects in seasons of focus. Perhaps your high school aged child needs Geometry, Biology, Government, Composition, World History, and Spanish this coming school year. That is quite a workload! Rather than bog them down with all of that at once, you could set up their learning in chunks that focus on 2-3 of those subjects at a time.

You could have them focus on Geometry, Spanish, and Government and work 5 days a week in each of those with no other distractions from other subjects. You let your child work at his or her own pace, or you guide them through a lesson plan you've created. Either way, the idea is to concentrate on only a few subjects and then move onto a few more.

CHAPTER 11

Focused seasons could be a semester long or less (I would not encourage longer than a semester). As a parent, you will need to make sure you do not add unnecessary work to their load, and help them to clear their schedule of anything that will hinder them from staying on track.

You can use this for any age! Try focusing for a season on getting your new reader fluent or your jr higher through that science text they've been dragging their feet on.

It is also great incentive for the child who wants to get a move on. My oldest child is currently working at breakneck speed through Geometry so he can get ready for taking some college courses.

Chunk learning has been the perfect answer to my time issues in our homeschooling. I'm able to redeem some time during the course of the week and still manage to fully teach what my children need to know.

CHAPTER 12

Training Toward Independece

CHAPTER 12

If you read nothing else from this book, this would be the one chapter I would beg you to read and work toward implementing. It will change how you homeschool and even how you parent. You are raising adults.

Soak that in for a second...

Children should not stay children, so as they mature and grow, you have to slowly start letting go of their hands and letting them take the lead on their own. And if they don't start taking the lead, you start pushing them toward that independence and responsibility they so desperately need to learn.

The Bible tells us we are raising arrows (Psalm 127) and arrows are meant to be launched. You craft them and hone them for that purpose. When you start giving your children independent homeschool work, you are training them toward the independence they will need as adults. You are giving them opportunities to practice within a safe environment where mistakes can happen without dire consequences.

Now before you ask me to give you an age by age account of what your child can be doing independently, let me stress how independence is not something that comes at certain ages. It is very much a case-by-case thing. You must know your child, how far to stretch them, how much they can handle and when. Don't expect the same things from one child to the next.
So rather than offer some nifty chart, I'm going to offer ideas and suggestions that you can use to formulate your own

Training Toward Independence

independence plan.

Workbooks
A great way to start implementing independent learning is via workbooks. Even before your child is a full-fledged reader, you can give them workbook-oriented tasks that are short and easy to follow. Walk away and come back to check progress. Are they doing what you asked? Are they taking an appropriate amount of time to complete their work?

If need be, give instructions again and repeat the process. Remember to start small and work your way up to more lengthy instructions, more pages, etc.

Then, when you feel they are ready, begin to give them the day's workbook assignment and let them do it on their own. Once you feel they have that under control, let them navigate the lessons on their own and mark what they have done on the lesson plan once they have completed each lesson.

Computer-based programs
Most computer-based programs have a built-in accountability to them. All you really need to do as a parent is check to make sure the work is being done and their grades are reflecting mastery of the subject.

Begin by giving them guidelines of how much work you expect to be done each day and then gradually move to each week, then each month, and eventually give them an ending date for

CHAPTER 12

the entire subject and let them budget their own time.

Special projects
As your children mature and find interests of their own, let them pursue those interest as homeschool subjects. For instance, my oldest son is very interested in World War 2. I told him that I would give him a credit in World War 2 history if he created a unit study on the topic. Doing so required him to research, know the material, and understand how to present it. It was a special project completely independent of my direct supervision. It allowed him to take his knowledge of a topic and run with it in a measurable way.

Other examples of this would be to have your child enter contests, work on projects from 4-H or Scouts during school time, create something to present to younger siblings or grandparents, or be in charge of a family project. The possibilities are endless!

But, perhaps you are reading this and thinking,
"My child doesn't work well on his own!"

Some children seem to balk at the notion of working independently. This can be very frustrating to a parent who is trying to either redeem some time for other children or desires to see their child gain some personal responsibility for his or her school work. However, it is important to recognize what might be the real reason your child doesn't work well on his or her own.

Training Toward Independence

They are scared of getting something wrong.
If you have always micromanaged your child's work, venturing out on their own will be very scary. They might be afraid you will check mark everything wrong or they will have to redo work they've completed. They prefer to have you by their side, helping them through so they avoid any mistakes and possible consequences for those mistakes.

These children need to be encouraged with baby steps and a mama who isn't overly critical of their attempts at independence. Start small, work your way up.

The work appears to have no purpose.
Some children are hyper-aware of "busy work" or work that has no direct impact on their lives, whether real or perceived. These children will balk at working independently because they don't really think the work is necessary in the first place. When asked to do work on their own, they will start it, but fail to complete it because it seems meaningless to them.

These children need to see how the pieces fit. You will need to get them "on board" with their school work and understand yourself why they need to do the work you are asking them to do.

They are socialites.
Some children don't like independent work because, well, it's independent. These children are your socialites who would rather talk through all their lessons than be set off by

CHAPTER 12

themselves to complete the work on their own. They see independent work as a punishment rather than a reward for being responsible.

These children need to check in with you. Give them independent work that is followed up with a "conference". Let them talk you through their work after they've completed it, and you can also give your input during these conferences.

By the time your child is ready to graduate from your homeschool, they should be able to handle their school workload on their own. They should know how to budget their time to complete tasks. They should know the proper order in which to complete tasks. None of this just happens. It must be nurtured and taught over the years by a parent who is purposefully raising adults.

CHAPTER 13

Keeping Track of It All: Planning & Record-Keeping

CHAPTER 13

If I had to choose the one homeschooling conversation I tend to have over and over with other homeschooling moms, it would hands-down be the "homeschool record-keeping" conversation. Frankly, it is not my favorite conversation, but it sure does keep a lot of moms up at night.

Tonight, I hope you rest easy...

Know your homeschooling laws
Before you ever begin to try to keep track of homeschooling, you need to know what exactly you are required to keep track of. States vary from super strict to super lenient, so be sure to check out your state laws via a reliable source such as HSLDA.org.

Decide how you want to keep track
I live in a state where the laws are not very strict, so my keeping track will look quite different from homeschool moms living in Pennsylvania. Once you know your state's law, you can make a more informed decision about HOW you are going to keep track of your school year. From one mom to another, my biggest piece of advice is:

Don't make it harder than you have to.

Here are some ideas to choose from:
- **Attendance record** – Similar to public school, you keep track of every day school is in session, assuming your day is similar in hours to a public school day.

Keeping Track of It All: Planning & Record-Keeping

- **Homeschool Planner or software** – These can be in the form of paper files or computer files. The best ones are the ones that can be used over and over.

An extensive list of planning pages and software can be found on the Resource Webpage for this book. Reference Chapter 13.
https://www.raisingarrows.net/lfhresources

- **School Binder or notebook** – This is an easy way to keep track that doesn't require any forethought. After your school day, you simply write down all you've done that day that constitutes school. You WILL be surprised!
- **Assignment sheets** – Another easy way to keep track is to let your assignment sheets serve as your record. Put them all into a folder and call it good.

Now, that we've established how you are going to keep track of your year, let's figure out the day-to-day stuff. Remember, your methods will change as your family changes and grows. What works for a time may not work forever. These are a few of the things we have tried over the years, some with long-term success, others for only a short season.

More information about the following methods can be found on the Resource Webpage for this book. Reference Chapter 13.
https://www.raisingarrows.net/lfhresources

Large Family Workboxes - When my children were all 10 and under, I used a modified workbox method to keep track of their

CHAPTER 13

daily lessons. Each child had a crate with hanging folders that contained each day's lessons and velcro tabs that could be removed and placed on a chart to let me know the lesson was complete. This worked best for us when we were doing a lot of workbooks and other independent age-graded work.

Assignment Binders – These were super helpful when I was pregnant. They were small colored comb-bound binders with several pockets inside and an outside closure to keep papers from falling out. I would load each week's work into the folder with an index card listing the assignments for the week. However, once they wore out, I did not replace them because my oldest child was no longer doing any worksheets and my methods of homeschooling had changed to be less textbook oriented. However, at the time, they were a lifesaver!

Markable Assignment Cards - For a very short time following a move to a new city, I used this method to help my children work independently so I could work on unpacking the household. These assignment cards were laminated index cards on which I could write out assignments for the day by subject. I punched a hole in each one and connected them with a metal book ring. The idea behind the method was sound, but I did not continue to use it once our home was in order.

Quick & Easy Assignment Cards - When my 7th born had colic, this was how we rolled. This is a great method to use during those seasons of life when things are hectic or stressful. Basically, you take an index card for each child and write down

Keeping Track of It All: Planning & Record-Keeping

everything they need to do for the day, including any meal prep or chores you need their help with. They can check things off and show you their card throughout the day. This is a great method to use when mom is unable to be up and around due to morning sickness, illness, or the newborn stage. This is also a good method for dad to use!

Planning Software - For many years, we used a planning software called Scholaric. My older children took care of their own lessons and marked them down in this web-based program. My current planning systems can be found in my book Flexible Homeschool Planning.

Plan to plan
When you plan your homeschool lessons will depend upon your current season. With the dynamics of our family, I prefer to not plan more than a week at a time; however, there have been times in my homeschooling career that have caused me to only be able to plan each individual day as it happened.

My ideal is a weekly planning session on a weekend evening, with a cup of coffee, sitting at our dining room table. The seasons when I am able to do this I find to be the most coordinated and stress-free.

What homeschool papers should be kept?

Short answer:
Only keep the really important stuff.

CHAPTER 13

Large families often struggle with the issue of how much to keep when it comes to school things. It would be easy to end up with boxes and boxes of papers by the end of your homeschooling career if you don't choose now to take the minimalist approach.

Here are my guidelines as to what makes it into that precious "School Keepsakes Box" I keep in the basement:

- Was it a momentous occasion? – Was it the first time Junior wrote his name? Was it the first essay Susie wrote that actually made sense? Was it a project that had been slaved over and finally accomplished? Those things are box-worthy.
- Does it show progress? – I try to keep papers and worksheets that show definite progress from one year to the next or from one task to the next.
- Will I be sorry I didn't include it? – The shapes book my 6 year old made isn't nearly as important to me as the All About Me book he made the same year. I won't miss the shapes book, but I would be very sorry to not have the book that tells me all about his likes and dislikes, dreams and aspirations as a 6 year old.

Another large family tip pertaining to the School Keepsakes Box - label everything with a name, age, and date. I put everything in one box, but even if you separate out into individual boxes, you will want to remember exactly what age they were. You can

Keeping Track of It All: Planning & Record-Keeping

also use that nifty Keepy app I mentioned in a previous chapter to reduce some of the items that go into the School Keepsakes Box.

The Extra Stuff

CHAPTER 14

Lighting Fires

CHAPTER 14

Education is not the filling of a pail, but the lighting of a fire.
~W.B. Yeats

If you have been a reader of Raising Arrows for very long, you know our family tends to put outside-the-box homeschooling far in front of traditional schooling methods. We choose to make the extracurricular intra-curricular and we are typically rather creative with our schooling. This kind of methodology stems from our theology. We believe a child's education is not meant to make them rich so they can retire happy. We believe true wisdom comes from knowing the Lord and all aspects of a child's education must be subject to the Lord's leading. We believe in lighting fires so that learning continues long after we are there to guide their hearts and minds.

Here are some quick out-of-the-box ideas for lighting fires:

Working alongside Mom & Dad
So much can be learned by working WITH someone on a project or even in everyday duties. Our children will all run households of their own someday and will need to know what it means to live life as a man or woman who seeks after Christ in all he or she does.

This requires patience on the parent's part because children are not always going to live up to your dreams and expectations. However, we know that what God calls you to, He will equip you for, and you can LEARN patience. Take the time to mentor your children because all the book-learning in the world cannot take the place of a truly interested and loving parent walking alongside a child.

Real Life Learning
As homeschooling parents, we need to take knowledge and "plug it in to something." Our children need to know WHY they are learning what they are learning and how it fits with the ultimate goal of knowing, loving, and serving God and loving and serving others. We need to seek out ways to make what they learn tangible and relevant.

Entrepreneurships
In the spirit of plugging a child's knowledge into a real life scenario, entrepreneurships are a lost method that must be brought back! Our children need real life application in a career field before they commit to years of study and work in that field. I'm not an advocate of wasting time and money, so I would much rather waste a little bit of time and money upfront to give my children opportunities to make informed decisions.

Field Trips & Vacations
I grew up going on vacations that were edu-cations so this has been something that has come naturally to our family. Even when my husband and I go places without the children, we tend to visit museums and other historical and informative sites.

When you have a large family, it is often much nicer and easier to go on field trips without a huge group of people along. Years ago, I quit going on organized field trips with homeschool

CHAPTER 14

support groups because it often resulted in utter chaos. I'd rather take my time with my own children, guiding them through the field trip without competing with their friends and a lot of extra noise.

Delight-Directed Extras
I have been a big fan of delight-directed homeschooling ever since I read Gregg Harris' book The Christian Homeschool. Think about how you learn as an adult. You are more apt to study and research and grow and learn when you want to know more about a subject that truly interests you. Your children are the same way, and since God has wired each and every one of them differently, it is so very important we study our children and learn who they are and what makes them tick. This is one of the beauties of the homeschooling environment! Don't squander it trying to fit into the box.

Multimedia
This is the place where I tell you not all media is bad. In fact, it can be an awesome learning tool, especially for children who are visual learners. My children have learned so much about Ancient Egypt and the Crusades and even how to make maple syrup from multimedia sources. We listen to CDs, watch DVDs, and use computer software like World Book on CD-ROM on a daily basis. The technological age does not have to be something that warps our young people's minds. It can be harnessed and used for good if we are always diligent to keep it in check.

Lighting Fires

The Resource Webpage for this book contains links to more posts on using technology in your homeschool. Reference Chapter 14. https://www.raisingarrows.net/lfhresources

For the large homeschooling family, the idea of lighting fires really comes down to knowing each of your children and what may or may not spark their interest. This might feel like an impossible task when you first begin to think about it, but I assure you, it will turn into an exciting treasure hunt!

So, tell yourself:
This year I will encourage interests.
This year I will stretch minds.
This year I will engage hearts.
This year I will disciple.
This year I will point the direction.
This year I will lead the way.
This year I will look for mastery.
This year I will wait for understanding.
This year I will take longer.
This year I will listen more.
This year I will laugh.
This year I will light fires.

CHAPTER 15

Extra-Curricular Activities

Extra-Curricular Activities

In Chapter 3, I told you the majority of the activities our family participates in are things our entire family can enjoy together. Initially, most people nod their heads in agreement at this statement, but if you really think about this statement, it is quite counter-cultural and might even make you a tad bit uncomfortable.

Why? Because it means you might have to say no to some things.

When there are many members in a household, it quickly becomes apparent that you cannot stretch your time to fit 10 different schedules. You have to consolidate and condense. Extra-curricular activities are one of the first places you should look when trying to redeem time with your family.

Don't just do things to do things
Outside activities for members of your household must be put under close scrutiny before you allow participation in them. Just because the local homeschool coop offers a certain class that sounds like fun or your best friend suggests you put your children in an activity she has her children in, does not mean you NEED to do it. Never should you do things just because you can or because someone else tells you you should. Busyness without purpose is a waste of time.

Here are some guidelines to help you evaluate your current and future activities so you are not stretching yourself thin amongst activities that do not truly fit the well-being of your family.

CHAPTER 15

1. Is the activity God-honoring?
There are lots of things to do out there; however, not everything is glorifying to the Lord. I won't try to discern for you what is and is not glorifying, but I will suggest this verse as a starting point:
Finally, brethren, whatsoever things are true, whatsoever things are honest, whatsoever things are just, whatsoever things are pure, whatsoever things are lovely, whatsoever things are of good report; if there be any virtue, and if there be any praise, think on these things.
Phil 4:8

Be honest in your evaluations of the activities you are involved in and be certain they honor our Creator, in whose image we are made.

2. Does the activity have "lasting merit."
The extra-curricular activities your family members participate in need to have lasting merit. This means the lessons they learn from the activity will be something they can use for a lifetime. Again, be honest. Don't grasp at straws trying to find even the slightest example of lasting merit to justify an activity. If you have to make excuses for the activity, it probably isn't something worth participating in.

Don't spend precious time doing the lesser things when there are so many better activities out there. A good question to ask yourself is:

Extra-Curricular Activities

"20 years from now will the fact that a family member participated in this activity prove to be beneficial to them or someone else in a tangible way?"

3. Does the activity correlate with the family member's particular giftings?

God has blessed each and every one of us with gifts that can benefit the body of Christ. We should pursue excellence in those giftings. We strive to hone the gifts our children were born with in order to "train them up in the way they should go." (Prov 22:6)

This goes for adults as well as children. If I had a knack for arranging flowers (which I don't), our family might consider it wise for me to take a class on floral arranging, make up arrangements to beautify our church, and further that aspect of myself in order to give of myself in my particular gifting (and possibly pass that knowledge on to other family members in the process). However, much of this could be done without me being away from my family for very long at a time. Anything that would take a family member away quite often and for several hours/days on end would need to meet the next criteria...

4. Does the activity benefit the family?

An example of this is my husband's hunting. If you read my blog, you've probably taken note of the buffalo hanging on my wall; however, my husband doesn't hunt in order to bring home trophies. That buffalo provided us with a freezer full of meat...low fat, high iron organic meat. Sometimes it is a deer,

CHAPTER 15

sometimes it is a pheasant, but his policy is don't hunt it unless you plan on eating it. And that's what we do. Therefore, that particular activity, now also enjoyed by our oldest son, benefits the family.

5. Does it encourage family-togetherness?
As you can see from my examples above, not everything we do is done as a family; however, family ALWAYS takes precedence over all else. If an activity shows signs of tearing away at the family, it needs to go. If you are spending more time apart as a family than together, you will begin to lose family unity – something no family should be willing to sacrifice. Always look for the unified family version of an activity before signing up for the separated family version.

Now, let me offer the flip side of this. Here are some things you should NOT use to choose your extra-curricular activities:

1. Is it fair?
If I spent my entire life trying to make everything fair for every member of my family, I would be a crazy lady and our household would run a muck. Fairness is not a good way to make decisions because you will likely end up with 2 or 3 places to be per child per week, which totally goes against #5 on the list above.

2. Peer pressure
Just because a friend is doing it doesn't make it right for your family. That doesn't necessarily mean the friend is making a

Extra-Curricular Activities

poor decision, but you can't choose activities based solely on what your friend or your child's friend is doing. For example, if my friend has decided to invest thousands of dollars in scuba lessons and equipment for her son because he intends to be an underwater archaeologist, it would be ludicrous for me to invest that kind of money on my own child, who more than likely has no interest or gifting toward that line of work. Make decisions based on your own family, not someone else's!

3. What the child wants
OK, that sounds harsh, but hear me out. Most children have two types of desires...those that are in line with gifts they possess and those that are not. My daughter may really, really, really want to take gymnastics and really, really, really want to take photography classes; however, I shouldn't feel compelled to give her both simply because she wants both. The Bible clearly states children are foolish. Guide them to good choices, avoiding willy-nilly choices based on the whim of the day.

CHAPTER 15

{Note from Amy - What about music lessons & sports?}
When the topic of extra-curricular activities comes up, most people automatically think music lessons and sports. There are some very strong opinions on both sides of this issue.

There is no way I can straight-across-the-board condemn or raise up one over another. My husband paid his way through college on a football scholarship. I had a music scholarship. My husband hasn't played football since. I sing all the time. His football benefited the family, my singing had lasting merit. It's a wash. So, rather than saying certain activities are ALWAYS bad and certain activities are ALWAYS good, we go back to our list. We work our way through it, prayerfully. At the end of the day, your family is your family, and the activities you choose to engage in do not have to meet anyone's standards, but God's. Go to the Lord in prayer about what HE would have your family participate in. Then do it wholeheartedly, as unto the Lord!

CHAPTER 16

Large Family Fun!

CHAPTER 16

In this day and age, having a large family is often equated with either irresponsibility or a lack of concern for the environment – both of which are nowhere near the truth. Having a large family also seems to invite comments...not all of them kind or even rational. The rude comment of, "Don't you know what causes that?" makes me want to scream..it makes my husband nod and smile.

A few years ago, we took an excursion to the grocery store...all of us. My husband was zipping up and down the aisles with the children strapped into those car carts I won't ever let them ride in when it's just me, while childless bystanders counted heads over and over, trying to figure out just how many of us there were.

Finally, one of them, a young woman in her early 20's, had the courage to speak to our crazy bunch. She said to me,

"You sure have your hands full."

Never heard that one before, but she said it good-naturedly, so I don't mind. And then she followed it up with,

"But you sure look like you have a lot of fun!"

Now, you're talkin'!

Large close-knit families who appeared to be having a blast together were one of the first things that drew my heart toward

Large Family Fun!

the idea of allowing the Lord to be in charge of our family size. I don't ever want to lose sight of the "fun" aspect of being a large family, especially when it comes to our homeschooling.

Make your studies fun.
Homeschooling does not have to be drudgery. There is no need to be all work, all the time. Spice up your school work with everything from stickers on their workbooks to parties! Make a box into a Reading Cave, have a picnic for lunch and then spend some time cloud-watching for science, dance to music and try to hear all the different instruments used. Allow learning to flow from the fun you have as a large family.

Ask your children what they enjoy about homeschooling.
Several times a year I gather all the school-aged children and ask them to tell me some of the things they like and dislike about our current homeschooling experience. I will often hear, "Remember when we...". Those are my clues to find more opportunities to do those things they deem to be memorable and fun.

Not everything has to be fun about school, but some of the best learning occurs when it is interlaced with enjoyable activities, and often some of the smallest things equal fun in children's eyes. So, ask them!

Be spontaneous (even if you have to plan it!)
Take a break from the studies and go outside, play a game, or take a field trip. One of the great things about being a large

CHAPTER 16

family is that there is almost always enough people to do just about any activity you can imagine.

And what looks like spontaneity to your children can actually be a well-thought out plan. There are nights when we get everyone jammied up and act like they are going to bed, only to make an ice cream run or a Christmas lights tour. Mom and Dad knew these things were coming, but no one else did, so they seem like fun by the shear fact that none of the children expected it. You can plan this kind of thing into your school day without telling the children and it will seem doubly fun to all involved!

Remember these children are blessings.
Blessings are fun! Whenever you start to feel worn down, take a moment to step back and really see what the Lord has given you. Take a break from homeschooling and take time to enjoy being the blessed mother of many!

CHAPTER 17

Affording the Large Family Homeschool

CHAPTER 17

For any large family seeking a private Christian education in the home, money quickly becomes an issue. While programs like K12 and other public-school umbrellas exist, they do not offer the freedom of choice and autonomy most homeschoolers are looking for. Nor do they offer a Christian education.

Most large homeschooling families opt to buy their own curriculum so they can be fully in charge of their children's education, thus making curriculum buying an exercise in creative frugality!

Here are a few ways you can save and stretch money in your homeschool:

1. Buy supplies in bulk.
Whenever you can, stock up and purchase in larger containers! You do this with food, why not with homeschool supplies? Places like Discount School Supply have great deals on large quantities of school supplies.

2. Use your library.
Many libraries now have their complete catalogs online. You can see what is available, request items, and plan out an entire school year based on what your local library has to offer.

3. Utilize free sites.
There are entire websites devoted to offering free curriculum like Ambleside Online, Old Fashioned Education, and Easy Peasy All-in-One Homeschooling. Free curriculum websites are

Affording the Large Family Homeschool

amazing resources that often use public domain materials to pull together comprehensive lesson plans. If you go this route, I would highly recommend investing in some type of eReader or tablet so your children are not confined to staring at a computer all day.

There are also a lot of websites now dedicated to alerting you to any homeschooling freebies on the web. The easiest way to take advantage of these freebies is to sign up for the website's newsletter so it comes to your inbox and you can choose from there what you would like to explore for you children's education.

There are also some really great unit studies available online for free. Homeschool Share is a great resource for this type of learning material. I would also highly recommend searching Pinterest for free resources.

Another great free way to homeschool is via YouTube. The History Channel has entire programs listed there and science experiments abound as well! The content on YouTube is amazing, but it also must be carefully monitored. Do not let your children randomly search YouTube. I would encourage you to create a document or Pinterest board with specific links to the videos you would like your children to watch rather than using the search feature on the YouTube home page.

You could easily pull together a full curriculum for all of your children with all the free stuff on the internet. It would take a

CHAPTER 17

little diligence, perseverance and time, but it is definitely doable.

4. Dream big and one at a time.
Most homeschool moms go into their school year with a budget in mind. They say things like, "I have $500 to spend for the entire school year. How can I get the biggest bang for my buck?" I would like to encourage you to come at your budget in a little different way.

Rather than seeing your children as a collective, look at each child individually and their individual interests and needs. Include the things most people consider "extras" and dream big. You can always pare down from there.

For instance, we've decided our youngest children only need Phonics and Math. The rest of their schooling can come from books we already own, library books, or living life. We focus the bulk of our budget on our older children and the increasing our own library of resources.

I start high with my homeschooling dreams and work my way down when deciding on a reasonable amount to spend each year. I write down each child's name and all the items I think they could use in a year and the price of each item. From there, I start paring down and searching for online resources to replace some of the items until I land on a more reasonable number.

Affording the Large Family Homeschool

Dreaming big for each individual child teaches you to see each of your child's strengths and weaknesses and interests in the context of education and discipleship. You may find yourself very surprised and very excited by the prospects of budgeting this way because it gives such insight for each child.

5. See your purchases as an investment.
This is the number one thing I tell homeschooling parents of many. Your purchase today will be passed down from one child to the next. If there is a curriculum you think would benefit your homeschool, but the price feels too hefty, don't always walk away from it. Consider how many of your children will be able to use it and other places you can scrimp in order to purchase it. The money you spend now will be well worth it in the long run. Several years back, I purchased a rather expensive phonics program; however, I have used it successfully with 3 children, making the cost much more reasonable.

And I want to urge you to realize your child's education is not just about academic scores. Homeschool parents have to move beyond test scores and textbooks as their measure of success before they will be able to homeschool with freedom and true success in the eyes of our Lord and Savior.

Other ideas for affording your homeschool year:
- Ask for certain items as gifts from grandparents.
- Sell some of your old curriculum via local homeschooling book fairs or online sites.
- Borrow or barter from another homeschooling family.

CHAPTER 18

Feeding the Crew

Feeding the Crew

One of the most challenging things for me as a large family homeschooling mom is feeding 3 meals a day plus snacks day in and day out to a rather large and diverse group of people. At any given time, I have teenagers, toddlers, and babies – all with different palates and needs. So, including a chapter in this book on meals seemed pretty important.

Let's start at the top o' the morning:

Breakfast is not my forte. I like to eat it, I hate to cook it. I've never been bright-eyed and bushy-tailed in the mornings. I can remember as a youngster never feeling as if I had fully awakened until about 10:30 am. I always wondered why teachers thought math needed to be taught first thing in the morning when I was so very tired. I try to have things on hand that can easily become breakfast, but rare is the occasion that I actually cook a hot breakfast. *GASP* Now, you know my secret!

Feel free to cook a big ole hot breakfast if this is your thing, but in case it isn't, here are some **breakfast ideas** - Amy style!
cereal
fruit
toast with peanut butter
hard boiled eggs
muffins
breakfast cookies
yogurt
baked oatmeal - prepare the night before

CHAPTER 18

fried eggs
leftovers

Next is lunch. By this point, we have been going strong with school and I almost hate to stop for nourishment! Lunch happens here between 12 and 1 pm – or whenever there is a natural lull in our school day. Occasionally, Daddy joins us, but most often, we are a table for 8. We typically have a light lunch rather than something heavy for two reasons:
1.   Our big meal is at night when Daddy is home.
2.   It is better and simpler to make something that takes less preparation when in the middle of a school day.

Here are some of our favorite lunch ideas:
pizza or lunch loaf using our homemade quick and easy pizza dough (The recipe is at the end of the chapter!)
bagel sandwiches
quesadillas
taco salad
cheese slices, crackers, and fruit
sandwiches
nachos
egg salad & chicken salad
leftovers

After we've cleaned up from lunch, we head back into our school day. If I were pregnant, this would be Rest Time, but as it stands right now, only the baby is taking a nap right after lunch.

Feeding the Crew

Our school day is usually finished around 3:00 pm. This is when I try to serve a snack to my hungry crew.

Snack ideas:
cheese & crackers
fruit
fold over peanut butter sandwiches
veggie sticks
smoothies
cookies

After snacks, I usually send the kiddos outside to play. If it is a nice day, we will often have our snack outside to reduce clean up. After we have played outside for a while, I head inside (usually with a helper) to prepare for supper/dinner.

We eat supper between 6 and 7 pm due to Daddy's schedule. This is typically our biggest meal of the day since Daddy is home. This is also the meal I am most creative with. I like to go through cookbooks and my index box full of the recipes I've been collecting for over half my life and pull interesting recipes I would like to try or bring out longtime family favorites.

Some favorite supper meals:
Italian Pot Pie
Winter Soup
Large Family Style Pot Pie (The recipe is at the end of the chapter!)
Bierocks

CHAPTER 18

Cheeseburger Casserole
Chili

Menu Planning Basics
As a mom of many, I have found that meal planning is the backbone of my day. Without it, I never feel in control or on top of things. I always feel like I am scrambling, hurried, and stressed. In fact, I feel so strongly about this that I would encourage you to take a look at your meal planning FIRST if you are feeling overwhelmed by your life right now. Get the backbone in place and work from there.

Over the years I've followed many different methods of meal planning. There is no right one, but there are some basics that will help you pull together a plan that works for your family.

1. Choose where you will get your recipes from.
Sometimes I use cookbooks I have on hand, sometimes recipes from my recipe binder, but lately, I find most of my recipes are coming from my Pinterest boards.

Many large family moms keep rotating meal plans so they don't have to think too much. You can also utilize a static pantry list that translates into several different meals.

2. Sit down and focus (or try to).
Sometimes I can knock out a menu in an afternoon. When planning several weeks, it can take me several days to get the whole thing finished. The key is to try to sit down and really

Feeding the Crew

focus; however, I know in a large family this is nearly impossible! If you can, have a big kid or your husband watch the children for an hour or so while you try to pull together your menu plan as quickly as you can. Make your environment as distraction-free as you can (that includes internet distractions) and pound it out!

3. Write in pencil (or the equivalent).
It's a given - your menu will change due to unforeseen circumstances. Our stove stopped working a while back and I had to revamp our menu to reflect this. Often, we have unexpected guests drop in and I need to rob a larger meal from another day to be able to feed everyone.

Your menu plan cannot be set in stone, so write it in pencil, or the equivalent. I say the equivalent because I now use Evernote, a web-based notebook to plan all my menus. It's not pencil, but it is easily changed.

When you need to erase or substitute a meal, simply put it onto another day or put it at the bottom of your page so you know you have that meal available for another time.

4. Make notes as you go.
Remember, this is the backbone of your day. Your meals are a direct reflection of your life. Write in notes about your day on the menu plan itself. Write down what days you have music lessons or other extra-curricular activities. Mark when you have company coming. Make notes to yourself like "order Azure" and

CHAPTER 18

"make ranch dressing", as well as things like "thaw hamburger" and "soak beans" in the appropriate places. Having these little notes is KEY to making your meal plan work.

5. Make your grocery list as you go.
Don't wait until you are finished with your menu to go back and input all the groceries you will need. Do it at the same time you are making your menu. Find a recipe, list it in a good spot on your planner, scan ingredients and mark down what you need.

When I am shopping monthly, I use a Master Grocery List that helps me keep track of staple items as well as new things needed to make the meals on my list.

An older version of my Master Grocery List can be found on the Resource Webpage for this book.
https://www.raisingarrows.net/lfhresources

When I am shopping weekly, I put my grocery list in Cozi, an on-line app that will sync with my husband's phone so I can input what I need and he can shop for it after work.

6. Plan everything!
Plan your sides, your snacks, even your beverages! If you do a Special Night with your children, put it on there. Don't forget potluck and family reunions. Do your very best to pull together a "backbone" that can withstand the pressure of your day, your week, and your month!

Feeding the Crew

7. Stock up on basics.
It is important to know the staple ingredients your family uses on a regular basis, and keep those on hand at all times so that even a crunch, you could pull together a meal. It's a good idea to "over" buy these items every trip to the store (or every other trip), so that you never run out.

This is one benefit of having a Master Grocery List and keeping track of your pantry, freezer, and refrigerator on a regular basis. You can even delegate this responsibility to an older child!

8. Look at your menu plan every day several times a day.
Keep your menu plan on your refrigerator or computer or beside your favorite chair. It has to be in a prominent location where you will be able to glance at it over the course of the day to be sure you are on track. Do you need to get something out of the freezer for tonight? It's on there! Need to prepare for a coming birthday? It's on there! Again, this is your backbone for the day. Using it to its full advantage is necessary!

CHAPTER 18

On Raising Arrows, there is an entire page dedicated to Large Family Recipes. http://www.raisingarrows.net/large-family-recipes/

Here are a couple of recipes to get you started:

Quick Pizza Dough
2½ c. flour
1 Tbsp yeast
1 tsp salt
4 Tbsp oil
1 c warm water
1 Tbsp honey
Preheat oven to 375°. Throw it all in the mixer with a dough hook and "knead" for 4-5 mins. Let rest for 5 minutes while you prepare the toppings. Roll out into two medium pizzas (rectangle shaped will get you more slices), add toppings and bake 12-15 mins. You have pizza in half an hour!
Topping ideas:
- Tomato sauce with Italian seasonings and garlic
- Canadian bacon
- Pepperoni
- Hamburger or buffalo burger
- Onion
- Green pepper
- Cheese
- Almonds
- Artichoke hearts
- Chicken
- Black olives

Feeding the Crew

Chicken Pot Pie Large Family Style
For crust:
2 c. whole wheat flour
4 c. unbleached flour
2 tsp baking powder
1 tsp salt
1 c. cold butter
2 c. cold water
In a large bowl, combine flour, baking powder, and salt. Cut in butter until crumbly. Gradually add water until dough sticks together. Turn onto floured surface and knead 10-12 times until smooth. Set aside 1/3 of the dough. Press remaining dough into 2 9×13" casserole dishes.
For filling:
6 c. cooked chicken
3 c. shredded cheese
1½-2 lbs mixed veggies (I use frozen)
2 cans cream of chicken
16 oz sour cream
1 onion, diced
1 small can of green chilis (if you have it and like it)
Mix together in large bowl and spread over crust.
Then, roll out remaining dough and cut into strips and lay over filling to form lattice-work.
Bake at 400° for 50 minutes.

The Other Stuff

CHAPTER 19

Caring for Yourself (and What About "Me Time"?)

CHAPTER 19

I appeal to you therefore, brothers, by the mercies of God, to present your bodies as a living sacrifice, holy and acceptable to God, which is your spiritual worship.
Romans 12:1

Years ago, I wrote an article called The Me Time Myth. I never expected the backlash I received over this article. I felt the ones who gave me a good tongue-lashing (even going so far as to suggest my children would hate me one day for NOT taking Me Time) truly did not hear my heart in the matter. I felt terribly misunderstood, but chose to avoid strife and stand quietly by my message.

When I chose to bring this topic up again on my blog in 2012, I did so with trepidation and trembling before the Lord. I wanted to include the essence of this message in this book because I feel it is an important one, especially for moms raising a large family and homeschooling. If you would like to read the original article, you may do so here:
http://www.raisingarrows.net/2009/07/me-time-myth/

As I see it, most homeschooling moms of many fall into 3 camps when it comes to the all-encompassing term "Me Time". They either live for it, piously deny themselves of it, or feel guilty if they get it. Very few seem to have a healthy view of this hotly debated issue. Today, I hope to shed some light on my original intentions with The Me Time Myth as well as what I see from Scripture as the way we should approach this topic.

Caring for Yourself
{and What About "Me Time"?}

Me Time shouldn't be the air we breathe.
I once overheard a woman tell her friends she could not live without her daily excursions to the gym where she could be without children and in her own space with her own thoughts. Suggesting you cannot live without Me Time is absurd and altogether frightening.

As mothers, we are called to love our husband and love our children. (Titus 2:4) Some suggest you cannot truly love these people if you are not first loving yourself. They talk of filling yourself first so you can fill others. But nowhere do I see that precedent in the Bible. In fact, I see the opposite. I see Scriptures about giving of yourself and caring for others ahead of your own needs.

Me Time should never be our lifeline. It should never be something we live for or try to get more of. It isn't commanded by Scripture and should not be taught as such.

Me Time Martyrs
However, there are those who staunchly proclaim their superiority because they have NEVER done anything that even remotely resembles Me Time. They decry anyone who goes to women's retreats or on vacations sans children. They rail against everything from bubble baths to curling irons to Starbucks coffee.

It's not the denying yourself I have a hard time stomaching. It's the pride. (Galatians 6:4) If you have to tell everyone how noble

CHAPTER 19

you are, are you really noble?

The Guilty Moms Club
My heart goes out to these moms. They are trying to do the right thing. They truly love their families, but they are weary and need encouragement and strength to keep going. At the very heart of the matter, they love homeschooling, they love being around their children, but they have off-days, off-weeks, and yes, sometimes even off-years. They long for a better life. They long for a peaceful home surrounded by happy faces and cheerful hearts, but they just cannot seem to make it work.

So, they hide.

They escape into Me Time every chance they get. But they know it doesn't satisfy and they feel guilty...oh so guilty.

A healthy view of me
The Christian mother has an opportunity to die to self daily as she learns to love her husband and children. The Christian homeschooling mother of many often finds this opportunity amplified. She may even feel as though she is forced to die to self because of all the needs that cry out for her every moment.

The answer to her struggle for more time, more energy, more joy is not to have less children or to stop homeschooling or to immerse herself in Me Time.

The answer is worship.

Caring for Yourself
{and What About "Me Time"?}

Romans 12:1 – the verse at the beginning of this chapter – sums up why Me Time is a myth. The sacrifices I make should never be about me. The time I spend away from my family should never be about me. The causes I support, the blog posts I write, the friendships I make should never be about me.

They should always be about Him.
I can carve out time away from my children for a coffee with my husband because I am there to rejoice in a marriage that daily shows the goodness of the Lord. I can spend a weekend at a conference with friends because I'm there to proclaim the glory and honor of Jesus Christ in friendships. I can even take a bubble bath with candles and soft music because I am there to pray and bask in the abundant blessings He has given me.

Moms, I want you to know it is okay to take care of yourselves. It is okay to stay at home and it is okay to go out. It is okay to exercise and okay to take a break. The thing you must always keep at the forefront of whatever it is you do is that this is NOT about YOU. It is about worship.

On the next page, you will find the Mom's Sacrifice List. It is a list of things you can do to take care of yourself so that you are presenting to God a sacrifice that isn't merely hanging on by a thread, but rather is a LIVING sacrifice.

CHAPTER 19

Mom's Sacrifice List
a daily checklist for being a living sacrifice to the Lord

Wake up at a reasonable time
Brush hair
Brush teeth
Wash face
Get dressed
Drink water
Take vitamins
Read Bible
Pray without ceasing
Take breaks
Go outside
Exercise or exert energy
Do something special for your husband
Do something special for your children
Go to bed at a decent time

CHAPTER 20

Homeschooling with Morning Sickness

CHAPTER 20

The large family mom is often homeschooling through rather difficult circumstances, one being morning sickness. If you are one of those women who never has experienced the awfulness of morning sickness, feel free to skip this chapter and count your blessings. For the rest of us, this chapter is here to offer hope and grace in the midst of your morning sickness storm.

- **First off, give yourself a break.** Morning sickness is not for the wimpy. It takes a lot of energy to lie on a couch and try to convince yourself you will survive. In fact, it takes a lot of energy just to make it to the couch in the first place (unless of course, you spent the night there). So, give yourself permission to take a break from all things.

- **Make things as simple as possible.** Plan easy meals, enlist someone to help you with laundry and dishes, and utilize paper plates, cups, etc. as much as possible. Get your husband to shop for you and keep the refrigerator stocked with easy snacks for you and the children. Don't be afraid to ask for help. You can be superwoman some other time.

- **You can catch up later.** One of the many beauties of homeschooling is flexibility. Is there really a need for you to stress right now about what is not getting done? Think about the larger picture. Will it really matter that you did not do 2 months worth of math with your 3rd grader when you can make up those 2 months somewhere else? Older children can keep up with many of their studies on their own and with very little direction. The short amount time you are

Homeschooling with Morning Sickness

sick (I know it feels like an eternity when you are in the midst of it), will even itself out in the long run. It will be okay. I promise.

> *{Note from Amy - Homeschooling Year Round}*
> *Morning sickness is one of the big reasons we homeschool year round. I know I can take off a couple of months because I'll be able to make it up some other time throughout the year. I am not beholden to a schedule that takes off in the summer, so I can redeem morning sickness down time during other months. This is definitely something worth considering for the large family homeschooling mom.*

- **Avoid "Bad Mother Syndrome".** I am convinced that my children are the most unruly, my house the most messy, my world the most chaotic, and I am very, very afraid I will never, ever feel "normal" again. It is during these times that it is most crucial for you to ask for the Lord's guidance. Sometimes, these feelings are a good "jumping-off" point for us to truly analyze our shortcomings and those we see within our families, but we also must be aware that Satan will use these times when we are already down and out to knock us down further and convince us we are no good at this Christianity thing or this homeschooling thing. He will put questions into our heads like:

"Wouldn't they all be better off if I just sent them to public school?"

CHAPTER 20

So, even in the midst of your illness, you must ask the Lord for discernment. Ask Him to show you TRUTH and give you the ability to PERSEVERE.

- And finally, when you do come up for air and realize the morning sickness is beginning to subside, **REJOICE!** Then... take a moment to look around you and **do the next thing.** What one thing that slipped while you were "away" should be re-established right away? Do you need to take some time to get the discipline of the children back under control? Is your husband begging you to clean the house and have all the laundry done up? Is everyone hungry for some "real" food?

Do not despair...what fell apart while the couch held you hostage will not take all that long to rectify with a little bit of consistency.

So, as a final note, let me say as someone who has survived morning sickness many times and who has homeschooled through a majority of those times, I empathize completely with your plight. It is a very difficult place to be. I hope you find some encouragement and hope from this chapter!

CHAPTER 21

Homeschooling with a Newborn

CHAPTER 21

I have homeschooled with a newborn no less than 6 times, so I feel "fairly" qualified to speak on the topic of homeschooling with a newborn. I say "fairly" because homeschooling with a newborn is always a brand new adventure since each of your babies is a brand new person!

PREPARING FOR A NEW BABY
For me, those final weeks of pregnancy are not incredibly productive ones. I'm one of those pregnant mamas who slows down everything at the end. I just can't keep up. School goes down to a bare minimum, and I take that extra time to prepare for what we'll be doing after baby is born.

We all know what we need to do to get our house ready for baby, but do we know what we need to do to get our school ready? Let's talk about the things you need to consider and prepare for when it comes to homeschooling with a newborn.

What Will School Look Like Before, During, & After Baby?
With Baby #8, I decided at 34 weeks to quit schooling until after baby arrived. Some of that decision had to do with it being Christmastime and some of that was just the fact that I knew I couldn't keep going at full speed.

Some mamas keep going right up to the end, and then choose to take their break AFTER baby is born; however, that's not me. Two weeks after baby arrives, I'm back at school again, not because I feel I have to, but because I love it that much!

Homeschooling with a Newborn

Speaking of "have to"...please, oh please, do not choose what your schooling will look like during these weeks out of GUILT. You are bringing another human being into the world. Take the time you NEED.

If you have older children, you might need to consider if they will continue to work on school work while you are having the baby or if they are able to take a break. It is my firm belief that young children do not need nearly the number of school hours we foist upon them, so I never have them do school when there is a life situation that keeps me from being by their side.

Because I birth in a hospital setting, our children stay with grandparents. Rarely do I expect grandparents to orchestrate school for the older children, and it is a pain to pack school books to take with them, so my children, big and little alike, typically get a break from school while Mama is having their newest sibling.

Getting Your Homeschool In Order
As I said above, after a couple of weeks, I'm ready to get back to school, so I like to have a plan in place for what school will look like in those early days and beyond. I bookmark sites on the internet and put them into folders, print off papers and put into files, reorder and organize supplies and books, and generally try to make the homeschooling part of my life as easy as possible.

Once baby is here, I typically focus my energies on getting the older kids started back into their work several days or even

CHAPTER 21

weeks before I get the little kids back into theirs. This gives us a chance to work through a new routine (more on that in a bit) and gives me more freedom.

It's okay to rely heavily on workbooks, videos, and audios in those early weeks. Make a list of some easy homeschooling materials you can use while you adjust to a new baby, and start preparing now for what school will look like then.

An Arm's Reach Away
This is my rule for everything when it comes to a new baby. It is also my homeschooling rule, newborn or not. I refuse to spend my time running all over the house for things I need. As I mentioned in the Organizing chapter, I keep a Nursing Mama Basket next to my chair. I use the same concept to create a Homeschooling Mama Basket.

When you are homeschooling with a newborn, you truly need everything to be as efficient as possible. Having the things you need most all within arm's reach makes life so much easier!

One Room Schoolhouse {literally}
Do school in one room. In fact, do school in one chair. OK, not everyone in the one chair, but YOU in ONE chair the entire time. You've got your Homeschooling Mama Basket for a reason! You do not need a table to homeschool.

Really, you don't.

Homeschooling with a Newborn

Choose a room. Choose your spot. Then, gather everyone there and save yourself a ton of energy!

Additionally, do as much as you can corporately. Now is the perfect time to switch to as much group work as you can. This means living books, discussions, unit studies and the like. In fact, you may find you love this type of homeschooling so much, you never go back!

Newborn-friendly Meals
If you manage to make up freezer meals or have family and friends bring in meals, fantastic! However, there's a good chance you'll run out of meals long before you are ready to jump back into cooking full time. Now is the time to plan some super simple meals that fit seamlessly into your homeschooling day. We'll talk more about these in a moment.

Take Care of Yourself
Nourish your body and brain as you prepare for baby's arrival. It took me 8 babies to realize I needed to take better care of myself, especially at the end of pregnancy. I've been known to subsist on candy bars and soda at the end of pregnancy because I'm tired...tired of being pregnant, tired of being fat (where's the logic there?), tired of being tired. I wish I could go back and do it all over again with the mindset I have now! What you eat now WILL make a difference in how you feel after!

THE FIRST WEEKS OF HOMESCHOOLING
Baby has arrived! You are elated, emotional, and exhausted...all

CHAPTER 21

day, every day. Now is not the time to stress over homeschooling!

Take a deep breath, and let's talk.

Baby Steps
Sometimes the upheaval of having a new baby can cause moms to want to create even more upheaval. We want to revamp our entire world. Frankly, I believe this is a hormonal reaction and a search for some sense of control and normalcy, but we have to give ourselves permission to slow down and take things to their lowest common denominator for a while.

When it comes to homeschooling with a newborn, you have 3 choices:
- No school
- Bare minimum school
- Back to normal school

In my opinion, it's best to follow these in order and move to the next one when you feel ready, and not a moment sooner. Start by telling yourself you have permission to take off from school while you adjust to a new baby. When you feel stronger, add in the bare minimum, namely independent work the children are capable of doing on their own or with minimal help from mom. This will give you time to work out kinks in your day, and find a new routine (*more on that a further into this chapter!*). When you are ready, you can step into your {new} normal school day.

Homeschooling with a Newborn

When Will I Find the Time to Homeschool?
We all know caring for a newborn takes time. We all know homeschooling takes time. We have 24 hours, and somewhere in there we need to sleep and eat as well. It's a balancing act, for sure!

Those newborn days may not follow your usual homeschool schedule and that's ok. You are allowed to wait until baby's nap to do school. It's ok if you do school in starts and stops. Let your children know things are going to be a bit different for a while, but do not make baby out to be a burden! Your newborn is a blessing and your other children will be blessed by the new baby in so many ways! Do not let workbooks and tests get in the way of being a family!

Ultimately, you find the time to school when you have the time. These newborn days are short and soon baby will have his own little schedule and you will find your rhythm.

Don't Do What You Don't Have to Do
You are not superwoman, and no one expects you to be either. More than likely, you are your own worst critic. Your expectations of yourself are too lofty for you to reach, and you need to let go of the guilt and only do what you need to do.

This is going to look different for everyone, based on your own convictions, passions, energy level, and time. One of the first things to go for me is bread baking. I'm okay with buying my bread in a store and saving myself those hours. One thing I

CHAPTER 21

don't let go in those early days is cloth diapering (although I will let it go when I'm dealing with morning sickness) because I really enjoy it! You have to choose what you can and cannot do, always remembering this isn't a permanent choice.

How To Homeschool AND Feed the Kids
Major events in my life tend to shut down my kitchen. I don't feel like cooking, dirtying up the kitchen, or cleaning up, but I still have to feed my children (remember Chapter 18?).

The best way to homeschool with a newborn and manage to feed the kids all in the same day is to simplify, simplify, simplify!

Breakfast - Whatever you choose, make it something the children can get on their own. Yogurt, fruit, peanut butter or honey on toast, granola, and cereal are all good options here.

Lunch - I'm a big fan of what we call Amish Lunches. These are simply individual finger foods that come together as a sort of free-form meal. To accomplish this, all you have to do is have some of these things on hand:
deli meat
cheese
crackers
pickles
jams & jellies
bread
fruit
veggies and dip

Homeschooling with a Newborn

hard-boiled eggs
nuts

Lay everything out and call it lunch! My kids love this, and it is oh so easy!

Dinner - Make this meal repeating and easy. Choose 7-10 recipes your family really likes and repeat them over and over. Good recipes for this category are:
Chili
Crockpot Hamburgers
Easy casseroles
Grilled sandwiches
Soups

And don't forget to feed yourself! Have an end table or tray table near your favorite chair so you can have a place to set food and a drink while you feed the baby because babies are hard-wired to wake up and need to eat the moment mama gets ready to eat.

A NEW ROUTINE
A new baby changes things. And that's ok.

Some changes might be subtle, while others can be dramatic. This can also depend greatly on the personality of the new baby and how members of the family relate to the new little one. There have only been two times in my life that adding a new baby has completely knocked me flat on my face: Baby #4 and

CHAPTER 21

Baby #7. Baby #4 came just 16 months after Baby #3 (something I had never experienced), and I quickly learned that all my routines had to change. Baby #7 was colicky and the tone of the household was greatly affected by that.

Frankly, every baby presents a new dynamic to the family and changes the routine of the household. So, before you try to jump back into "normal," watch your life for a while to see where "normal" needs to change.

For instance, our last baby didn't change our normal much at all. He's an easy-going baby, and we were pretty much able to pick up where we left off. However, the baby before that changed our daily schedule dramatically. He was only happy if he was nursing or being held by his older brother, who was 13 at the time. My oldest would do school while I nursed the baby and did what I could from the chair, then he would take over and I would work with the other children. We'd switch again, and I'd sit in the chair and we'd do read-alouds and have history discussions, and then I'd nap with baby in my arms because sleep was hard to come by.

Those days looked nothing like the "normal" I was used to, but I had to let go of that normal and embrace the new routine. The sooner you let go of the ideal, the sooner you can find your new routine and be satisfied with it.

Work From Where You Are
I want to clarify something here...

Homeschooling with a Newborn

A tightly woven schedule is rarely doable when homeschooling with a newborn. In my ebook, The Homemaker's Guide to Creating the Perfect Schedule, I talk about Schedule versus Routine families, and how to tell which one you are, and then work with those natural tendencies to create a schedule that works for you. During those newborn days nearly EVERYONE would consider themselves a ROUTINE family rather than Scheduled because of the changes and adaptations the family is undergoing. If you try to schedule out your day in 30 minute increments, you will be a crazy woman before the morning is over. You have to look for a NEW Routine that works for you.

I give a lot more detail in the ebook, but the quickest way to get started figuring out your new routine, is to write down the routine you have naturally fallen into since baby's birth and work from there.

So, if baby wakes up at approximately 7 am every morning and nurses, and then other children wake up, and breakfast gets started, and eventually school gets going, and then baby needs to eat again, and so on and so forth, you use that routine to build your new routine. Don't write down exact times, but rather the ORDER in which things are happening.

Relish those Newborn Days
I want to take a step back from all this scheduling talk and give you my heart. I used to race through my children's baby days. I'm efficient to a fault, and I just wanted to get on with it already. As I've gotten older, and I'm by no means old mind you, I've

CHAPTER 21

begun to really slow down and savor tiny toes, fuzzy hair, and the beautiful chaos of babyhood. It's gone before you know it, and I don't want you to miss it.

More than Muddling
So often, new moms just muddle through. We are surviving moment to moment, and we hope and pray we survive it all. That doesn't sound much like an abundant life, does it?

Come to me, all who labor and are heavy laden, and I will give you rest.
Matthew 11:28

If ever there was a verse for moms homeschooling with a newborn, this would be it! Come to Him! Stop trying to do and be it all and rest. It's ok if you fall asleep in the middle of a read aloud. It's ok if you stop what you are doing to nurse the baby. It's ok if you don't follow all the lesson plans to a tee and don't do everything the Teacher's Manual says you have to do.
rest.

Go to Christ, take your children with you, and rest in His Holy Word. If you get nothing else done in those early weeks besides family devotions, the Lord will bless your faithfulness.

He loves you, and He did not give you this precious reward of a newborn baby in order to make your life difficult. He gave that baby to you to bless you. So, BE BLESSED!

Homeschooling with a Newborn

HELPERS, BIG & SMALL
So, we've talked a lot so far about what YOU can do, but how about getting some help?! That's right, homeschooling with a newborn requires help!

Let's talk about what I call the "small helpers" first. These are divided into two categories:
Ready Made and **Home Grown**

Ready Made Helpers
Years ago, I read a blog post where the author called baby paraphernalia "baby containers." While I do think there are parents who rely too heavily on swings and walkers and the like, most homeschooling parents I know are not neglectful, and would never put their child in a "container" in the hopes that they would not have to deal with them.

So, with that said, I want to encourage you to get the ready made help you need to homeschool with a newborn.

Here are some examples of Ready Made (or Mama Made) items that can be a huge help to your homeschooling efforts:

1. Wrap, Mei-Tai, Sling, Backpack, etc.
I started slingin' babies when my 3rd child was born. These are a great tool when you need to hold baby, but still need your hands free.

I started out with a Maya Wrap inspired sling I made myself, and

CHAPTER 21

later moved to making my own Mei Tai wraps. Most baby wraps are easy to make, but even if you aren't much for sewing your own, it is still a good idea to own one or two baby carriers.

On the Resource Webpage, you will find posts and examples of baby carriers.
https://www.raisingarrows.net/lfhresources

Homeschooling benefits:
- Your hands are free to help other children.
- Most babies find the act of being carried quite soothing.

2. Snugabunny Rock 'N Play Sleeper

This piece of baby equipment has been one of my favorites! It is a cozy, sleeper that is elevated on rockers. It folds up easily and takes up very little space. This has become our main sleeper for baby.

Homeschooling benefits:
- Lightweight and portable.
- Allows baby to be in the same room with you all the time.
- Baby can use it to sleep or "play" during school hours.

3. Playpen or Bassinet

There are a million of these to choose from! We use our playpens as beds for older babies and toddlers because they don't take up as much room as a crib. But, a playpen or

Homeschooling with a Newborn

bassinet set up in the main homeschooling room can be a nice safe place for baby to be during school hours.

Homeschooling benefits:
- Easy to set up and take down.
- Keeps baby safe from little hands.

4. Swing

There are some wonderful infant swings on the market right now. The ones that swing from side to side are my favorites. There are even swings that can be plugged in to save you on batteries.

My colicky baby would only sleep in my son's arms or his swing, so we purchased a portable swing to take with us to grandparents' houses. It was a lifesaver!

Homeschooling benefits:
- Often soothes a very fussy baby.
- Provides a 2nd "bed" for baby that is in the main homeschooling space.

5. Bumbo Seat

Not every baby loves the Bumbo as much as my youngest child did, but I must say the use it got with him was well worth the price I paid for something baby tends to use for only a short time. I've shared my Bumbo with friends too so I don't feel bad

CHAPTER 21

about spending the money.

Homeschooling Benefits:
- Lightweight and portable
- Keeps an older baby engaged with the family
- Protects baby from being stepped on!

6. High Chair that leans back

A few years ago I would have told you this was a waste of money, but one thing we cherish as a family is our time spent around the table for family meals. We like baby to be a part of that, and while the Bumbo allows baby to sit up, it leaves him on the floor. The high chair we own (see Resource Webpage) has height adjustments and a reclining seat so baby can sit with us for meal times. The same concept applies for any homeschooling done around the table. Baby gets to be right there in the middle of it all!

Homeschooling benefits:
- Baby is eye level with everyone
- Seat reclines to accommodate younger babies

Small Home Grown Helpers
These are the helpers you have in your home who are too little to be given major baby care responsibilities, but who are still able to help. In my home, these are the 2-8 year old crowd (in your home, this age range might be different).
What can the little ones do?

Homeschooling with a Newborn

- fetch diapers, blankets, and other needs
- "talk" to baby
- "play" with baby

They may not be able to carry baby around, but they can be super helpful and super entertaining!

The Big Home Grown Helpers
My big helpers are currently 9, 13, and 16.

Some people take issue with older children helping to care for younger siblings, but this isn't about mom eating bon-bons while the teens do all the work. They are not my slaves. This is about giving my children opportunities to learn and bless others. It is my prayer they step into adulthood as prepared as they can be (because nothing really fully prepares you, does it?).

What can your big helpers do?
- Care for the baby while you are working with other siblings.
- Make meals (please, please, please teach your teens to cook!)
- Learn to work independently, thus cutting down on the number of people who need your direct supervision for school.
- Help teach concepts to younger children.
- Help set up fun activities for younger children.
- Be your "Teacher's Aide" by running copies, finding books, researching, and gathering supplies.

CHAPTER 21

- Keep things clean and running smoothly.

So many people complain about their teens. I love mine! And many people underestimate the abilities of younger children, but I totally consider my 9 year old a "big helper" because she is very capable and willing to pitch in wherever needed.

If you don't have a big helper in the house quite yet, don't hesitate to ask another homeschooling family if you can borrow one of theirs a day or two a week. However, be VERY clear about what responsibilities you need a Mommy's Helper to help with. Do you want her to play with the children while you work or work while you tend to the children's needs? Make a list if need be.

UNEXPECTED CIRCUMSTANCES
So far, we've talked about what homeschooling with a newborn looks like under normal circumstances; however, not every birth, baby, and postpartum goes smoothly. Sometimes events surrounding giving birth are less than ideal.

Until my 7th child, the only outside-the-norm circumstances I had ever experienced were 2 c-sections. While c-sections are often difficult to recover from, I was back to normal in 2-4 weeks, and thankfully, both babies were very good-natured. But, Baby #7 made homeschooling quite a difficult task. His pregnancy was difficult and drug on through a very hot summer. At 5 hours old, he began to cry, and he was 4 months old before he became the happy-go-lucky little boy he is today.

Homeschooling with a Newborn

Add to that the fact that the difficult emotions I dealt with during pregnancy followed me and became full-blown postpartum depression. I was a hormonal, exhausted mess caring for a fussy uncomfortable newborn. Homeschooling felt like an impossibility.

These are the times in life when you have to just let go. You can't control what is happening to you. You are not a failure, and there is so much that can be learned through crisis. The number one piece of advice I can give you when it comes to homeschooling with a newborn when circumstances are difficult is to hand it all over to the Lord, and trust that He will supply your every need…including your homeschooling needs.

"For my yoke is easy, and my burden is light."
Matthew 11:30

Some resources you might find helpful when those early days are not what you envisioned and you find yourself in the midst of a crisis can be found on the Resource Webpage
https://www.raisingarrows.net/lfhresources

CHAPTER 22

Homeschooling with a Toddler

Homeschooling with a Toddler

At the beginning of the homeschool day, the toddlers are playing nicely at your feet; however, 2 minutes into teaching square roots, and they have disappeared. An eerie calm overtakes the house. You hear squeaky laughter intermittently escaping from somewhere down the hallway.

You follow said laughter only to find all family members 3 feet and under sitting in the bathtub playing happily, covered in bubble bath.

And you wonder how you are ever going to manage to homeschool with toddlers in tow.

Here are my
Top 10 Ways to Corral the Kiddos During School Time

1. Sleep
No, not you - THEM! Put those babies down for a nap! This one works great when you have elementary aged children and younger. School does not take as long in those early years, so it can easily be fit into the toddler's nap schedule. For years we homeschooled at 1pm every day because that was when the toddler napped.

2. Play Pen
My toddler LOVES to keep his younger brother company in the play pen. No, it's not a cage, but hey, even if it was...what toddler doesn't love a cage?!

CHAPTER 22

3. Pretend School
Get your toddler his own crayons and "workbooks" just like the big kids!

4. "Quiet" Games
Gather up card games, bears & balancing buckets, clothespin games and file folder games - anything that is quiet and will keep them entertained for a bit. Get out one at a time and switch them out as soon as you see their interest waning.

5. Lauri Puzzles
These are soft foam puzzles just right for little hands and mouths!

6. Cardboard boxes
Need I say more?

7. A box of toys just for school time
It could be soldiers, it could be horses, it could be dress up clothes...but whatever it is, it is ONLY for school time!

8. Board Books
Not just for reading. My children create the most amazing "book houses" with their board books. You might have to show them how to do it once or twice, but after that their dolls and army men will be living in the lap of luxury!

9. Playdough & Paint
I just saw a couple of you cringe. Get washable paint and use

Homeschooling with a Toddler

a homemade play dough recipe, and I promise you, it isn't that bad. It could be worse…it could be glitter!

10. Let 'em run and clean up later.
Some days are just like that.

Several of these can be combined into what I call the **TODDLER BOX.**

This box is something I put together specifically for my toddlers to keep them busy during school hours. They can only get it out when we are having school and only in the same room.
What's in the Toddler Box?
- puzzles
- pipe cleaners
- alphabet stamps
- paper
- crayons
- cloth tape measure
- magnifying glass
- books
- anything I think would catch their interest for approximately 30 minutes at a time

Your toddler box doesn't have to be full of new and exciting stuff, it just has to be full of stuff! You could put cookie cutters and cotton balls, blocks and cars, sewing cards or a deck of cards in there.

CHAPTER 22

You will have to direct some of their play - especially in the beginning. You will need to ask them to use their pipe cleaners to make certain shapes or ask them to find you a yellow car, etc.

Don't overthink the Toddler Box - keep it simple and functional!

And finally, I want to speak to the one question so many homeschooling moms of many ask, especially in the early days...

"Does it get easier?"

At the age of 29 with four small children, I remember feeling worn out. Because I had all "littles" and no "bigs," the bulk majority of the household responsibilities rested with me. Sure, the children helped, but rather than "many hands make light work," it was more like, "little hands make more work." I wondered if things would ever get easier.

By the time I was 33, I had a 12 year old by my side, and I can truthfully tell you things do get easier. However, I know just how hard it can be to see the forest for the trees when you are standing in the middle of it all. You don't want to just muddle through, but that seems to be all you ever manage. You know there has to be a better way.

Even the moms-of-many who have older children have days of just muddling through, but there is a lot to be said for thriving, rather than just surviving.

Homeschooling with a Toddler

So, what can you do when you are a mommy of littles to make the most of this season?

Lower your expectations.
You look at other families or websites with all these children working and playing alongside each other and you wonder, "Will that ever be my family?" I remember the days of wishing the conversation around the dinner table was something more edifying and interesting than the baby crying and the toddler spilling her water for the third time. I longed for something that wasn't even possible for my family, and it made me sad.

However, when you lower your expectation of what things *should* look like, and focus more on where you are now and what you can do as a family now, you stop longing after the future.

Let your littles work alongside you.
Let them do less-than-perfect work. Play their silly games. Laugh with them and love on them. You are in a season of sowing seeds. Accept that the fruit comes later.

Implement what you can now.
In Chapter 1, I told you about how crucial it is to adopt a large family mentality from the beginning. This is probably the number one thing I did as a mom of only littles that saved my sanity!

I learned to implement a bath routine, a morning routine,

CHAPTER 22

shopping rules, table rules, and a myriad of other ideas I gleaned from moms much further down the parenting road than I.

Large families, by default, are efficient, and no matter what size or age your family is, gathering from their wisdom and putting it into practice before you need it, makes for a much smoother day.

The future is bright.
"All littles and no bigs" will not always define your family. When I was in that stage, I had an older mother tell me that by the time my oldest was nine, I would see a difference. Nine seemed a long way away, but she gave me hope.

Guess what?! She was right! My oldest child was a huge help by that time, and I could see the other children beginning to follow his example. It was exciting to see years of training pay off! So, never fear! Littles DO grow into bigs!

When it comes down to it, it is all about perspective. Enjoy where you are now, train for the future, love what you do. No matter how little or how big they are, you are blessed to be their mommy!

CHAPTER 23

Homeschooling During Crisis

CHAPTER 23

I've been married for 17 years. In those 17 years, I've had 8 children and 4 miscarriages. I've survived 2 deployments and 12 moves. I've held my father's hand as he slipped from this world at the age of 82, and I've handed my little girl into the arms of Jesus at the age of 7 months.

I am no stranger to crisis.

And I would venture to guess most of you reading this have had your fair share of crisis as well.

Before we go any further, I want to give you a working definition of CRISIS:
- anything that is outside of your norm
- that causes you stress
- for an extended period of time.

We encounter situations every day that are outside our norm, but they don't constitute a true crisis until they cause us stress and extend longer than a few days. These are the moments of our lives when day to day life must find us depending on God's mercies to survive.

When my husband was deployed, I had 2 little ones. Thankfully, I had family nearby to help pinch hit for me, but I remember clearly a day when I was sure I could not go on any longer. I was tired of being a single mom. I was tired of changing diapers, giving baths, dealing with everything needed to run the household, homeschooling my oldest, and doing this

Homeschooling During Crisis

day in and day out without my husband by my side. I was exhausted and depressed. I shut my bedroom door, flung myself on my bed and cried out to God to bring someone to take my children away for the day so I could breathe.

I'm not proud of how I felt, but it was how I felt nonetheless. And God is faithful, no matter how we feel. My mother-in-law just "happened" to stop by and offer to take the kids for the day. Through tears of thankfulness, I ushered my then 5 and 2 year olds out the door.

I also remember clearly the days of the couch holding me hostage as I tried to make it through one more day of morning sickness. 8 times, totaling 2 years of my life have been spent in this manner. (YIKES!) School comes to an excruciatingly abrupt halt and I find myself wishing I could just go to sleep and wake up around 20 weeks. It is a crisis.

And then there was the day my world changed forever. The day my daughter Emily went to be with the Lord. When Emmy was 5 months old, she suddenly became very sick with what appeared to be a very bad cold, but turned out to be a twisting and dying off of her small intestine due to an undiagnosed congenital defect known as malrotation. After 3 surgeries and 4 weeks in the hospital, we brought a tiny, exhausted little girl home to recover. A month later, while staying with friends, we awoke to Emily struggling to breathe. 2 hours later, in that small town emergency room, our little Emily closed her eyes and slipped from this earth and into her Heavenly Father's arms.

CHAPTER 23

We were devastated. The hardest thing I've ever had to do was hand my child's lifeless body to a woman I did not know and walk out the doors of that hospital.

The second hardest thing I ever had to do was to heal.

It was nearly 2 months before I felt like I could even attempt to look for something resembling normal in my life. That was 6 years ago, and as I have healed, I have determined to encourage and comfort others with the same comfort God has shown me.

This chapter is born out my own crisis. I pray it speaks to your heart, whatever crisis you are currently facing.

PREPARING FOR A CRISIS
Quick disclaimer. There is absolutely NO WAY you can fully prepare for a crisis; otherwise, it would not be a crisis. God allows trials in our lives to grow us and glorify Him. Oftentimes, the true depth of your faith will be made known during a crisis. And oftentimes, we come out of a crisis knowing more about ourselves and more about the God we serve.

The only reason I suggest preparing for a crisis is so that when, NOT IF, a crisis happens, you will have some things in place that will allow others to minister to you during this time as well as allow you to put your life on autopilot while you focus on the crisis at hand.

Homeschooling During Crisis

Go to the ant, O sluggard; consider her ways, and be wise.
Without having any chief, officer, or ruler, she prepares her bread in summer and gathers her food in harvest.
Proverbs 6:6-8

Proverbs 6 tells us to go to the ant and consider her ways. It is WISE for us to gather supplies in the summer of normal in preparation for the winter of crisis.

How to prepare for a crisis

Let me start by saying, the things I am going to suggest you do to plan for a crisis are things that will help your homeschool and your household here and now as well. They are ideas that will give you a more efficient, smoother-running home even in times of normalcy.

First, get a brightly colored folder and make that your Go-To Folder. It should be kept in a place that is easy to find and easy to direct others to.

Some of you may already have a Homekeeping Binder, but this is in addition to that. This is really just an emergency folder to keep all your important auto-pilot information in.

Next...

Create some Basic Lists

CHAPTER 23

These are the basic outlines of your daily life. All the things we've been talking about in previous chapters; the lists, the charts, the routines, go into this folder. Anything that would help someone else to run your household belongs here. Include the school subjects your children can do on their own and your At-a-Glance daily schedule.

Don't forget to include an easy meal list and a corresponding grocery list. This is basically 7 days worth of breakfast, lunch, and dinner consisting of VERY easy meals. Do NOT come up with elaborate meals that require brain power and long hours in the kitchen. Also, include any recipes needed for these meals, even the meals you don't think need a recipe. Taco Salad may be a no-brainer to you, but Grandma might not have a clue how this is made.

And lastly, include important phone numbers, allergies and social security numbers. If you are not comfortable keeping everyone's social security numbers in a folder like this, at least have a common place for them so if you had to call someone and ask them to look up a social security number for you, you would know precisely where to direct them to.

Start NOW to create a uniform day.

You don't have to have a rigid schedule, but you do need some sort of routine. Begin now to create an environment where everyone knows what happens when and what their role is during the day. When a crisis hits, this will be a security blanket

Homeschooling During Crisis

you can fall back on, especially if you have older children who know the routine and can manage the household well on their own. During a crisis you will probably not be able to create "normal" days, but the pattern of normalcy is in place so as you pull out of the crisis, you have a strong starting point.

Teach your children to own their work.

Reread Chapter 12.

Children as young as 4 or 5 can "own" their chores and children as young as 8 can "own" their school work.

When a child owns their work, they learn to be responsible for that work even when you are not there breathing down their necks. Yes, they will still need guidance for a good long while, but the younger you start teaching responsibility, the sooner you will have an independent worker that will require less of you in the way of chores and schoolwork during a crisis.

You can find the Age Appropriate Chore List in the Appendix.

Put together a Rainy Day list.

This is a great thing to have on hand, crisis or not. Think of it as your Autopilot School. List every puzzle, workbook, book, CD, DVD, online resource your children can use to learn during a crisis period.

CHAPTER 23

PERSEVERE THROUGH A CRISIS

Now that we have prepared as much as possible for a crisis, what happens when a crisis actually strikes?

Let go of the guilt.

Any one who has lived through a crisis can tell you there is guilt. You feel guilty for not doing all the things you think you OUGHT to be doing. You feel guilty over certain decisions, you feel guilty over certain indecisions.

Do not make your parenting and homeschooling decisions out of guilt or fear.

That said, crisis can make you a crazy person. Even now, my decisions are different since having a child die than they once were. Some of my decisions are made with the knowledge in the back of my head that children do die and things do go wrong. And that's just part of my "new normal." I have fears, but I also have the ability to choose to give those fears to the Lord. Guilt and fear will consume you if you do not consciously choose to hand that burden over.

Let your life go on autopilot.

All the things we talked about in the PREPARE section can now be implemented. Those schedules and meal plans and chore lists are there...USE THEM. Just as the ant in Proverbs stored

Homeschooling During Crisis

her supplies and then used them throughout the lean months, you have the supplies you need to go on autopilot in the lean/crisis times.

But don't feel as if you have to use them to their fullest capacity. Remember, we are not parenting by guilt or fear. Take what you can from your plans and let the rest go. If you only manage to do a few of the things on your list or cook a few of the meals from your menu, your preparations have been worth it.

Let others help you.

Neighbors, friends, family, your own children can and should be allowed to bless you during a crisis. Paul calls this "fruit that abounds." Do not hinder them under the guise of pride of fear of inconveniencing them or being a burden.

I remember feeling needy. An entire year of being needy. I went from having a child hospitalized to having a child die to getting pregnant and dealing with morning sickness to having a c-section. I wondered if I would ever be helpful or able to reciprocate to someone else. Yet, I realize now all those families who helped me and blessed me and my family were blessed in return for their faithfulness in giving to another in their time of need. They stored up treasure in Heaven on my account. I am humbled.

You will not always be the one in need. So, let others be there for you.

CHAPTER 23

Focus on Scripture.

If you do nothing else, teach and read the Word. God will fill in the gaps.

Philippians 4:6 tells us to *"be anxious for nothing, but in everything by prayer and supplication, with thanksgiving, let {our} request be made known to God."*

I have seen firsthand where my children have not done formal schooling during crisis, but when the crisis is over, the Lord has faithfully caught them up to where they needed to be.

Steep yourself in His Word so that the overflowing of your heart is Scripture. Speak it to your children, read it to them. Keep yourself grounded spiritually because I will guarantee you will find yourself dealing with hard spiritual questions when you are dealing with a crisis.

Now, we need to talk about how to...

PROGRESS PAST & HEAL FROM A CRISIS

Remember: Slow & Steady wins the race.

We have to stop seeing a crisis as a bump in the road that must be overcome as quickly as possible so we can get back to our regularly scheduled life.

Homeschooling During Crisis

This IS your life.

Take it as a gift from God, a growth experience, a chance to glorify and honor Him through it all.

Progressing past the storms of life take time. They are not something we should expect or even want to rush through. Yes, I know I said when I have morning sickness I want to go to sleep and wake up at 20 weeks, but the truth is I have to take it one day, one moment at a time…slow & steady. To everything there is a season.

Normal does not mean "the same."

When life begins to slow again, you will find yourself wanting normal immediately. And more than likely the normal you are wanting is the normal you used to have. Realize this will never be again. The crisis you have just endured has shaped and changed you…forever. Give yourself time to find a new normal and accept that new normal.

You can help create a sense of normal by creating some constants in your life…even if that constant is simply "at 4 o'clock we watch a movie." This is where your old schedules and routines will come in handy. Take pieces and parts of those old routines and begin to fit them into your new normal.

CHAPTER 23

3. Read through the Psalms.

Several years ago, I wrote a devotional for grieving families entitled, Psalms for the Grieving Heart. While it was written specifically for people grieving the death of a loved one, it has helped many people going through personal crises to connect with Scripture and begin to heal through the power of the Holy Spirit. You can find it on my blog as a free gift to grieving families.

Let others help you.
Again, I'll say it...let others help you. You will be able to reciprocate later.

Lastly...

Don't live in crisis mode forever.
1 Peter 5:8 says, *"Be sober, be vigilant, because your adversary the devil walks around like a roaring lion seeking whom he may devour."*

You are weakened when the storm of a crisis passes and that vulnerability can lead to temptations - temptations that will devour you. Be vigilant.

I also think it is important to say here that it is okay to have joy through a crisis. Having joy does not mean pretending this is easy or acting like you aren't hurting and it also doesn't mean you have forgotten the gravity of your situation. It simply means Christ's mercy and grace are all the more abundant. Appreciate the moments of joy you are granted.

Homeschooling During Crisis

When we are broken, Christ shines through. Being broken is humbling and scary. But there is One who has seen it all, experienced it all, so that we don't have to bear it all on our own.

EPILOGUE

What I Wish Someone Had Told Me About Homeschooling

What I Wish Someone Had Told Me About Homeschooling

Homeschooling lacks a map to tell you exactly what the path will be like throughout your journey. Below are the things I wish I had known before I set out on this journey.

You will never stop analyzing.
Every subject you teach, every method you use, every word you speak will race through your brain day and night. No matter how many homeschool conference speakers drill into your head that you truly are your child's best teacher, you will still question yourself and worry about everything from teaching your 6 year old to read to making sure your high schooler is complying with state standards. You will pray and research and pray some more, tirelessly looking for the best in everything you do. And this will never cease, even after your last child is long graduated from your homeschool. However, all this analyzing will make you a better mother because it will teach you to capitalize on your strengths and rely on God to fill in your weaknesses.

You will learn much more than you will ever be able to teach.
You will learn to love history because you homeschool. You will appreciate the world around you more because you homeschool. You will become a lifelong learner because you homeschool. And you will never, ever be able to impart to your children all the things you want to teach them. You will own piles and piles of books in which lie pages and pages of projects and information you want to teach someday...a day that will never come. And hopefully, you will learn to let go of your need to be everything to your children, finally

EPILOGUE

understanding you cannot possibly hold yourself responsible for teaching them everything they need to know. Besides, one day they might homeschool and learn everything you couldn't manage to teach.

You will own a massive collection of books.
Just face it now and buy bookshelves. Lots and lots of bookshelves.

You will want more books.
See #2. That's what happens when learning really seeps into your blood. You crave information and you get a high from buying books. The pen is mightier than the sword, so you desire to surround yourself with this strength.

You will start "safe" and end up eclectic.
Every long term homeschooler I know has a difficult time pegging themselves as a method homeschooler. You hear a lot of

Well, I'm a Charlotte Mason with a little Classical thrown in. Oh, and we do several unit studies throughout the year. Oh, and I'm really fascinated by the Delight Directed movement.

That's why so many of us veteran homeschoolers cringe when you ask the question...

What curriculum do you use?
We're afraid of scaring you. We know what we are doing, but we

What I Wish Someone Had Told Me About Homeschooling

remember well when we didn't, and we were scared by people who couldn't answer the curriculum question. But there will come a day when you will branch out and you will feel totally and utterly out of control, but it will feel good! Do not fear eclectic. Embrace it!

You will feel inadequate...often.
There is an entire world out there telling you you aren't qualified for this job. Let's get one thing straight before I say any more... that world lies. And the very fact that you question yourself, leads straight back to #1. Because you analyze and stress about your child's education, you are the PERFECT person to teach them! You actually CARE!

You will want to give up.
I'm going to level with you a second, I have never once wanted to put my children in government school. God called me to this and no matter how hard it is at times, I see no other way than this.
However, that isn't the only way homeschool moms give up.

Some homeschool moms want to give up on a certain child.

Some homeschool moms want to give up on their spouses.

Homeschool moms often feel alone in their struggles. They think they are the only ones who are going through what they are going through with a particular child or a spouse who doesn't play an active role in homeschooling. Some do see the

EPILOGUE

grass of government school as greener and some just drop the plate that seems to be spinning out of control, no matter the consequences.

This is where we must build a sense of community and then allow ourselves to depend on that community. Yes, it takes a lot of guts to tell someone you feel like giving up and it takes even more guts to hear their response, but we need to be told the hard stuff and we need to be a part of something bigger so we stop feeling like we are homeschooling islands.

Your kids will amaze you.
Need I say more?

Occasionally, YOU will amaze you.
I just love it when God hands me one of those Gold Star days!

You will cry…a lot.
Homeschooling is a huge gut-wrenching responsibility. It is also a tremendous blessing that will leave you speechless. The first words your child reads will be because of you.

The outbursts of frustration that come from a difficult math problem will be spewed on you. The daily ups and downs of life as a homeschooling family will primarily belong to you. You will cry tears of joy, tears of anger and tears of exhaustion. God will bottle those tears and bless you for your faithfulness and you will cry at the beauty of it all.
Even though homeschooling brings anxiety and angst and tears

What I Wish Someone Had Told Me About Homeschooling

aplenty, you will never regret being humbled and awestruck daily by the precious little children sitting round your dining room table (or all over the house, in my case). And someday when you wish someone had told you what homeschooling was really about, you will realize it doesn't matter. You are changed forever. For the better.

APPENDIX

Homeschooling Methods & Large Family Considerations

Homeschooling Methods & Large Family Considerations

When the large homeschooling family goes to research homeschooling methods, they quickly realize many of these methods do not take their unique family size and needs into consideration. Sure, taking nature walks every day the Charlotte Mason way sounds delightful in theory, but when you add in 2 toddlers, a newborn, and a tired mommy, it becomes an exercise in chaos.

When the large family chooses curriculum, they have to "consider the cost" and choose wisely. No method will truly fit your needs exactly, but nearly all can be tweaked sufficiently. Below, I've offered a guide to help you find a good homeschooling approach for your family and super-size it!

Traditional Textbooks & Workbooks
Description: Ready-made curriculum in the form of texts and fillable workbooks with teacher guides.

Pros:
- No major lesson planning required.
- Gives mom a concise list of everything she needs to say and all the supplies she needs to gather to execute the lessons.
- Can be given to the child as their own responsibility because everything is laid out in order.

Cons:
- Rarely uses living books that are interesting to the child.
- Lacks creativity; can be considered boring and dry.

APPENDIX

- Can sometimes be teacher-intensive.
- May be frustrating to both mom and child.

Tweaks:
Use in conjunction with other curriculum to offer a well-rounded and creative education that interests both mom and child.
Don't require children to do all the problems in the workbook or read all the pages in the textbook.

Combine children and subjects to cut down on how much time you spend teaching each subject.

Unit Studies
Description: Topical study that utilizes many different learning styles and methods to teach the subject and other inter-related subjects.

Pros:
- Can be tailored toward a child's or family's interests and needs.
- Combines many subjects into one learning venue.
- Many free online resources.

Cons:
- Gathering supplies and information can be time-consuming.
- Not all children are interested in the same thing.
- Some aspects of unit studies can be difficult for some children and/or mothers. (i.e. lapbooks, notebooking,

projects etc.)
Tweaks:
- Don't do all the projects.
- Choose unit studies that span many ages and levels.
- Add in books and videos to take some of the burden of gathering supplies off mom.

Charlotte Mason
Description: Living books and nature-study based form of education that takes a leisurely pace, often utilizing notebooks, narration and short lessons to imprint learning on the child's mind.

Pros:
- Well-suited to creating a close-knit home atmosphere.
- Often gives children a love of learning.
- Short lessons help to avoid burnout.
- Utilizes living books, leaving "twaddle" behind; thus, giving children an appetite for good literature.

Cons:
- Some aspects can be difficult for a large family to implement. (i.e. long nature walks, lots of notebooks, narration in the formal sense)
- Requires mom to be engaged in the learning process; thus making it difficult to implement during difficult seasons.
- Requires good management and organizational skills to keep a handle on books, notebooks, lapbooks, nature

APPENDIX

studies, etc.

Tweaks:
- Combine student notebooks, narrations, and lessons. We use Notebooking Pages for most of our notebooking needs.
- Implement the "essence" of Charlotte Mason without doing everything a smaller family might do. For instance, take shorter nature walks and rather than keeping a nature study notebook, keep a nature table with their treasures displayed for a time.
- Gather your own home library of twaddle-free living books to make access to these resources easier.
- Take a break during difficult seasons.

Delight-Directed
Description: Child interest-led study that digs deep into subjects of interest and allows for those interests to be utilized in other subjects.

Pros:
- Fosters a love of learning.
- Acknowledges each child's unique interests and personality.
- Makes learning fun.
- Gives learning "real world" application.

Cons:
- Requires parents to seek out opportunities for children to

Homeschooling Methods & Large Family Considerations

   pursue interests.
- Can easily "overwhelm" and overshadow other academic subjects.
- Is difficult to track.

Tweaks:
- Make delight-directed in-depth studies something the child does AFTER traditional school work is finished.
- Infuse traditional school work with their interests. For instance, a budding artist is allowed to illustrate essays and word problems, and embellish notebooks.
- Keep a journal of delight-directed studies to facilitate tracking of the studies. Or have the child keep a notebook of what they have been learning to give measurable results.
- Only do delight-directed studies during certain times of the year or certain months.

Principle
Description: Bible used as the main text and starting point for all other lessons and subjects.

Pros:
- The Word of God does not return void. (Isaiah 55:11)
- The Fear of the Lord is the beginning of wisdom and knowledge. (Proverbs (9:11)
- Acknowledges the Cornerstone of all academic studies.
- Is easily implemented with wide range of ages and abilities.

APPENDIX

Cons:
- Takes some creativity to implement as it goes against "conventional" schooling methods.
- Requires a very hands-on, open and available parent-child relationship where conversations characterize the school day.
- Tweaks:
- Start slowly with one or two subjects.
- Learn to start your day with in-depth Bible study.
- Utilize online resources to generate conversations.

Classical

Description: Teaching based on the 3 stages of child-development: Grammar, Logic, & Rhetoric - that implement classic literature and ancient models that give children a highly academic education.

Pros:
- Offers a well-rounded, college-bound education.
- Many available resources.
- Fosters reasoning and cognitive skills.

Cons:
- Can be extremely rigorous and intensive for both child and parent.
- Parent must be prepared to discuss difficult topics and present them from a biblical worldview.
- Can lead to burnout if not kept in check.

Homeschooling Methods & Large Family Considerations

Tweaks:
- Can enroll children in classical homeschooling groups to reduce the teaching burden.
- Look for classical curriculum that is taught from a biblical worldview.
- Skip lessons that are too intense or too difficult for the season you are in.
- Remember, lessons cycle, so if you miss something this cycle, it will come around again.
- Only implement with older children.

Unschooling
Description: Allowing the child to learn within their natural environment without the aid of curriculum and lesson plans.

Pros:
- Fosters a love of learning because children are able to pursue their interests and stay with them as long as they like.
- Does not require purchasing curriculum.
- Can be done anywhere.
- Can be beneficial to retraining government schooled children to enjoy the process of learning.

Cons:
- Can create anxiety that you are not doing "enough".
- Can easily lead to lack of parental involvement.
- Difficult to track.
- Difficult to explain to others.

APPENDIX

- Requires parent to facilitate learning environments.

Tweaks:
- Unschool only as far as you are comfortable.
- Keep a journal to track unschooling "lessons."
- Create opportunities for learning that work within the family dynamic and meet a family need. For instance, build something, research something, make learning a team effort.

CHERISH YOUR CHILDREN CHECKLIST

☐ **Greet them with a smile.** *(1 Peter 3:4)*

☐ **Disciple them in the ways of the Lord.** *(Deuteronomy 6:4-9)*

☐ **Pray aloud over them for their specific needs.** *(Colossians 4:2)*

☐ **Pray privately for their specific needs.** *(Philippians 4:6)*

☐ **Work alongside them. Play alongside them.** *(Matthew 19:14)*

☐ **Show your affection for them often.** *(Malachi 4:6)*

☐ **Praise them for wise choices and guide them away from foolish ones.** *(Proverbs 29:15)*

☐ **Discipline them out of love and concern for their well-being, not out of anger or in defense of personal feelings.** *(Philippians 2:3)*

☐ **Teach them to respect authority.** *(John 5:27)*

☐ **Model the character qualities you would like to see in them.** *(Titus 2:7-8)*

- [ ] **Give them responsibilities and have confidence in their ability to be responsible.** *(Matthew 13:12)*

- [ ] **Foster and direct their God-given gifts; teaching them to glorify the Lord with their talents.** *(Romans 12:1)*

- [ ] **Teach them to think outside the box, ever-focused on the Lord.** *(Romans 12:2)*

AGE-APPROPRIATE CHORE LIST

Any time I mention children's chores on the blog, I almost invariably have someone ask for an age-appropriate chore list or at least some idea of what ages are capable of what tasks. I typically shy away from this question because children are so very different; however, a couple of years ago, I decided I would try to put together some sort of list as a guideline, hoping everyone who read it would fully understand the unique dynamics and circumstances of their individual children.

This is NOT an exhaustive list. There is absolutely no way I could manage such a feat. So, take this list, tweak it for your family's needs, and let your children begin to demonstrate responsibility by helping around the home!

Oh, and a few very important items of note as you peruse this list:
- ALWAYS try to include your children in what you are already doing.
- Give them chances to lead.
- Respect their personalities and natural abilities while realizing the need to stretch and grow them.
- Don't give up! Teaching responsibility is a worthy goal and something our culture sorely lacks. Press on, mama!

9 – 12 Months
- help put away toys

-turn off lights, reach for towels, take out plastic dishes and/or cups and silverware for meals with your help, etc (as in you hold them and they reach with your hands guiding all the while)

1 – 2 years old
- help put away toys
- use proper "manners" with please, thank you, excuse me, sorry
- help with Tidy Time (be sure to give specific direction)
- help with bedroom chores like making the bed, putting dirty clothes in hamper, putting socks in drawers
- wipe down furniture with a rag
- help clean up their own messes (if they spill a glass of water, they can help by getting a towel and doing their best to wipe it up)
- simple errands like putting a diaper in the trash or picking up a toy for baby

2 – 3 years old
- drag laundry baskets to laundry area
- help sort laundry
- take their own dishes to the sink after meals
- wipe down chairs for Table Chores
- help with more complicated and specific errands (like being able to tell them to put a certain dish away in a certain cupboard without actually having to stand over them)
- guided help with putting away their own laundry
- help load cart and unload cart at grocery store and help bring in groceries from van at home
- begin helping with outside chores so they can see how things

work (essential if you are on a farm)

3 – 4 years old
- continue to expand chores listed above
- learn to make bed (this is the very reason we do not use top sheets – too difficult for little hands)
- learn to follow a morning chore list
- begin establishing regular chores like putting away outside toys before Daddy mows or dusting living room blinds with a static duster
- learn to get their own drinks

4 – 5 years old
- learn how to dust
- learn how to vacuum
- learn how to set the table
- learn where things are kept so he/she can dependably do "big" errands for Mommy & Daddy like getting trash bags or Spot Shot and junk towels
- learn to fold towels and put them away
- help with meal prep
- learn to water plants

5 – 6 years old
- make bed without help
- begin to help younger siblings with tasks
- be responsible for going-out items like the diaper bag or Bible bag
- begin doing cleaning chores and errands they learned

previously without supervision
- learn to fold all laundry items and put in proper places (ie laundry baskets or drawers or shelves)
- help with more complicated meal prep
- learn to wash dishes
- begin doing more serious outside work
- begin recognizing how they can be of help without being asked

6 – 7 years old
- wash dishes or unload dishwasher unsupervised.
- begin learning how to prepare simple meals and snacks
- begin learning how to do laundry from start to finish
- have inside and outside chores that are theirs to complete without supervision

8 – 10 years old
- complete responsibility for their domain (bedroom, specific chores, etc)
- unsupervised yard work
- begin being responsible for one meal a week and learn more complex meals
- tackle difficult cleaning and organizing projects
- begin contributing to the family's "think tank" by being a part of certain family decisions, financial planning, and logistics and brainstorming
- begin taking on paying jobs (whether outside or inside the home)
- begin learning "adult" tasks and chores like vehicle maintenance, handy-man jobs, and the creating of schedules

and routines

There is an economy of the household, especially in a large household. There is work to be done and children must be a part of this work. However, they also must see you working hard too. They must feel like they are part of something bigger and their part matters.

I know I have inadvertently left things off this list and I know I don't always get this list right, but I keep trying. I keep training. I keep raising arrows that I pray will one day be sharpened and ready to be responsible for their own households.

RESOURCES

Many of the chapters in this ebook require more information, photos, and links than could possibly fit within these pages. Because of this, I have created a page on Raising Arrows that shares the extras. You can access that page here: https://www.raisingarrows.net/lfhresources

If you know of any resources you would like me to consider adding to that webpage, feel free to email me at amy@raisingarrows.net.

If any blessing comes from this ebook, let the Lord Jesus Christ receive all the glory!

Amy Roberts
RaisingArrows.net

Printed in Great Britain
by Amazon